Reforming the Church

From a House to a Home

Keith B. Ferrante

Published by:
Keith B. Ferrante
6391 Leisure Town Rd.
Vacaville, CA 95687

Ferrante, Keith B. (2014-08-20).
Reforming the Church : From a House to a Home

Cover Designer: Paul Wayland Lee

Library of Congress Control Number: 2014915230

ISBN-10: 1500919101
ISBN-13: 978-1500919108

Table of Contents

Acknowledgments

I want to give an enormous thanks to Tom and Angie Parsons. Your joyful tireless efforts to edit, help structure, and help shape this book have made my writings readable and hopefully enjoyable. I am so absolutely thankful for the treasure you both have been to me through your efforts. Many blessings.

To David and Deborah Crone, Dan and Regina McCollam, and Gary and Karissa Hopkins for believing and encouraging me as I have journeyed with you all at the Mission. To the Mission staff, thank you for allowing me to be a part of a team that is looking to truly revive and reform the church to what it is supposed to be. You are such a dream team to be a part of.

Thank you finally to my lovely wife Heather and amazing children Maci and Micah for allowing me to journey with you towards something new and upgraded. Heather without you I'd have made some devastating messes in my attempts towards reform. Your wisdom and friendship has been a tethering point for me. I love you. Maci and Micah thanks for being adventurous children that have also said yes to the discovery of the hidden treasures of the deep places in God. My efforts to reform the present church into a greater expression of relevance are because of my heart to see you and the next generation expanding the Kingdom. If I can help push the parameters of the norm to encompass new territory maybe your lives will bear more fruit. I pray that my ceiling will become your floor and you both will journey into new and unknown territory to expand what God has given to you. Much love and blessings.

Introduction

The church is in need of reform. This is not about what is wrong with the church. This is about what is missing. God is upgrading the church because she has prayed crying out for a mighty harvest. He wants to give her what she is praying for. In order to give the increase there has to be a different framework for the blessings of harvest to come. There is no resistance on heavens side about this wonderful harvest that we have been talking about. God wants to pour out on us the answers to our prayers. We simply have to be able to get under the faucet of blessing if we want to see fruit for what we have been praying for.

Many people pray for harvest and wonder why it isn't there. That is why we need reformation. The church meetings, mindsets, paradigms, patterns, identities, views of God and relationships must be upgraded in order to facilitate what is coming from heaven. The blessing is absolutely waiting and I am convinced it is available for all who get in alignment with it. That is the good news. The challenging thing in all this is that we have to be willing to be uncomfortable and to change the very culture that we have operated within for the last few hundred years if we are going to see this. Those that embrace what God is doing will find the heavens open up over them and such blessings and fruit come down. Those that want to stick to the old patterns, however good they were, will find that the prophetic promises and answers to prayers long prayed keep eluding them. We cannot think that we can get different fruit while still doing the same things. The harvest we have in church life now is a result of what the previous revelations of God have created. If we want different fruit a different pattern is needed. It is the pattern of heaven; it is an unveiling of how heaven operates to another dimension and a broader understanding. Leaders of corporate church are going to have to be willing to embrace the change or resist it and find continually less life and more struggle in what they are doing. Most of us pray that our lives would make a difference and that we would please God in all we do. He wants to answer that prayer but sometimes it requires us to step into an area that is uncomfortable for us.

Over ten years ago I received a prophecy from a man while speaking at a meeting in London, England. I had an unusual encounter where I was immediately taken outside of the meeting I was in and high into the heavens. I was in the spirit realm and in that context he prophesied this book that I am now writing. This book has been brewing in my spirit for over 15 years and I've felt the urgency and grace to write it down in this season. This book is not a book full of new answers, but rather new questions. These questions and fewer answers are backed by the experience the Lord has shown me prophetically and practically about what is coming. I believe this book has markers in it if you receive them and apply them; they will catapult you into the next move of God. I believe many of us have received and are walking in revival manifestations. I don't believe this next wave is another revival. Revival means to awaken from a lack of life or restore life to something that was dead. I believe the move of God that is upon us is a reformation. A reformation is a restructuring of how things are done, how we think, how we see God, how we see others and how we see ourselves. This shift is needed so we can facilitate and welcome the next phase of heaven on earth. It is exciting and I pray you choose to embrace whatever learning curve is required to get there.

All of the things that I release prophetically come from a variety of experiences I have had with God and in relationships with other prophetic and apostolic people of God. Many others sense and are stepping into the reform of God. I am simply trying to communicate what I feel are the key elements the Lord has shown me over the last years of what the present move of God is supposed to look like. I in no way believe the things in here mark every parameter of the reformation upon us. These are simply the markers that I presently see relating to our present church structures and ways of relating. I know there are many other markers and many other people that carry other unique markers for reformation. I am so excited about all the changes that are upon us because I love to be continually changing and upgrading towards the full maturity of Christ in us. I think the full maturity of Christ in us will only be realized when we have fully integrated every character of God and every identity of Christ into our lives. Every arena of life must be saturated with the personality of heaven within us to create an authentic bride that fully manifests Christ on earth. We must take the things prophesied and move them from the spirit realm to the practical and physical realm. They must become a part of our every day interactions and must successfully function in and around us. Then and only then have we integrated the things taught until they are truly no longer just head knowledge but reality.

I bless you in your journey to reformation and pray God's blessings on you as together we discover a greater manifestation of heaven on earth.

Much grace and Courage,
Keith Ferrante

Keith B. Ferrante

Chapter 1

Reforming Leaders
From Preachers To Fathers

W ithin the next 50 years, we will see an extraordinary shift in how we manifest heaven on earth through the church. This shift became clearly defined a few years ago during a meeting I didn't want to speak at. For several years leading up to that meeting, I had been traveling as an itinerant minister. At the time, I had been enjoying a much-needed break from the intensive travels. Rather surprisingly, I was asked to speak in the youth group.

The Unexpected Invitation

I didn't have a problem with the youth at all. However, I couldn't see how this would be exciting for me, especially after spending several years on the road. I wrestled with my thoughts. Traveling as an itinerant minister was how I made my living, and this meeting would not provide any income. Additionally, there would be no selling of product to help others move forward or to build towards a greater expression of my ministry. A speaking engagement at any conference would not come out of that meeting. This meeting didn't seem to have any future advancement in it at all. Besides all that, I was just plain tired from the rigorous traveling schedule I had been on for quite some time. How could speaking to a bunch of youth be significant?

Now I know that I am being really vulnerable here and you may want to throw me under the bus if my vulnerability now confirms your suspicions. Suspicions such as, "all ministers want money" or "ministers don't really care about people." Honestly, I make my living as a vocational minister and that's how I keep food on the table for my family. I do love people and I believe that is realized in the way I minister. I know it may not seem "spiritual" to work as a minister, but I'm honestly trying to give you an opportunity to put this book down before I get too real.

WARNING
Reading Further May Be Hazardous To Your Comfort Zone

It may be too much to handle for some. But wait! That's the whole point of the reformation that is upon us. Ok, well I think I'll go on.

My immediate response to being invited to speak to the youth was, "No. What do I have to offer? I am past my effectiveness in youth." At the time, I was thirty-seven years old, had already been a head pastor for ten years and had been speaking in conferences, churches and ministry schools around the world for several years. It had been nearly fifteen years since I had been involved with the youth. I loved it way back then but it didn't seem like the right time nor place for the present season of ministry I was in. Honestly, this felt unconnected to the goals of my present reality.

I had just devoted six months delving into a vision to see supernatural schools in every nation, and the desire to see this happen was burning within me. How would speaking at a youth group help me achieve that? Reluctantly after all the inner wrestling, I said yes. Little did I know what God had in store as a result of my unenthusiastic yes.

Captured by God's Heart for Them

In preparing to speak with the youth, I asked God to give me a message. I was having a hard time getting my heart and mind wrapped around what I could possibly say that would be relevant to them. He responded, "Just get a heart for them like they're your own children." I have two wonderful children of my own, so I could relate to that. God said, "Would you want your children to have an encounter with God? Give them an encounter like they are your own children." As a Dad, I want more then anything to see my children encountering God in a powerful life-changing way. So I developed a message to bring to the youth with my children in mind.

I arrived at the meeting, prepared and ready to speak. I was as ready as I could be while still feeling disqualified and irrelevant. Would I be good enough? As I watched those young ones worship, the Lord unexpectedly began to move on my heart. My heart began to open up towards them. As I saw their passionate worship and hearts for God, my compassion towards them started to grow. My heart internally cried out, "God, these youth don't need another trendy youth pastor. What they need is a Father. God, give them a Father!" I prayed silently, but passionately. Little did I know how He would answer that prayer.

As I spoke that night, He gave me such a heart for them; or should I say He snuck His heart for them on me. He awakened a long lost passion for a group of people I was no longer looking to influence. It seemed like time just flew by. An hour after the meeting was officially over, we were still crying and weeping together as our hearts were knit together. I left the meeting continuing to pray, "God, give them a Father." I had been awakened to a passion that existed long ago in me for the youth.

3

But still I didn't really understand what had just happened.

A New Adventure Begins

Several weeks later, my senior leader David Crone and a few others met with me and asked me what I was passionate to pursue in our local church. He was setting me up, in a good way, but I didn't realize it at the time. They asked me some questions; what did I see myself doing at home? I responded with the standard answers - running the local church, worship, and a few other things, but nothing really seemed all that exciting at the time. Then, Dave asked me "Would you consider overseeing the youth?" My immediate thoughts were, "Not on your life. What do I have to offer? I am irrelevant. I'm too old and not trendy enough. I don't have time." Even after that wonderful youth meeting a few weeks before, I still couldn't read the writing on the wall. Initially I said no, but I have a heart to do what is right even when I don't feel like it. I knew underneath it was what God was asking of me, even though, at that moment, it didn't feel as significant as traveling to the nations, conferences, etc. After a few days of wrestling with the invitation I reluctantly said yes.

Just a Dad

More then two years have passed since that time. Initially I was just the overseer of the youth team, and was developing a youth pastor and an associate. However, through a series of unexpected events, I eventually became the "youth pastor." I use that title lightly because honestly, I don't see myself as a youth pastor. I am simply a dad who has a heart for these youth. I don't even go as far to consider myself their dad, but rather I just know I am a dad and when I meet with them, I let our time together flow from there.

When I first started, I preached many messages to them. They were great for the starting season and developed in me the mindset to begin to think as a youth. Currently, I don't try to preach a great fancy message for them, or even try to be cool, trendy or relevant to their age group. (I do realize that some of these things can have their place, however.) But I simply speak to them as I would my own children. I speak directly to the things I know they are going through. I try to keep my ear to the ground for what is going on with the youth by connecting with them and by listening to the group of leaders that directly pastor them. I don't try to be charismatic or even prophetic, but rather focus on their practical needs. What are they going through? What issues are they facing? Maybe I even use a bit of my prophetic intuition to determine what God wants to deal with, but I try to keep it to what the needs are that seem to be on the Lord's heart to address in their lives.

Spiritual Family Reform

Even though I am not focusing with the youth on releasing the prophetic ministry I normally operate in on a wider scale, I am functioning in the very heart of the prophetic seen in Malachi 4 when God says though Malachi,

> "See, I will send you the prophet Elijah before that great and dreadful day of the Lord comes. He will turn the hearts of the fathers to their children, and the hearts of the children to their fathers; or else I will come and strike the land with a curse."
> (Malachi 4:5-6)

This scripture captures how I am engaging with the youth. I don't have to try and perform for them; my heart is for them as a dad is for his own kids. I get to be who I am already, a dad with children.

I believe this coming reformation will devote more emphasis on fathering and less on preaching. Lately, I have had such a passion to focus less on developing a good sermon and have chosen to focus more on being a dad that shares life with those around. This has even extended beyond the youth group. If you are wondering if I am getting away from preaching, the answer to that is definitely not. Rather, this shift occurs in terms of the way we communicate. I am giving myself to communicate relevant truth that transforms. I am simply pursuing exploration of a different way of communicating the truth. There is certainly a place for pulpit preaching; it guides us, gives us encouragement, etc. However, fathering may be a key that unlocks a door to a culture that I don't think we have yet embraced on a wider scale.

A Shift in Fathering

All Fathers are preachers and teachers but not all preachers and teachers are Fathers. Maybe not all are preaching or teaching from pulpits, but their lives are living messages. Fathers operate from a much different place than preachers do. Preachers convey truth, inspire, train and exhort. Teachers teach, give tools, and help people understand difficult things in a simple way. Fathers use preaching and teaching to get a much larger task accomplished. This includes raising up sons and daughters to be successful in their purpose, secure in their identity and empowered towards their destiny. You normally need a pulpit to be a preacher, which eliminates many in the congregation. It's just simply a practical matter. We don't have enough pulpits and time to hear all the people that should be heard. But we do need all the people to know the Father and to begin to manifest the Father to those they would see as sons and daughters.

When reviewing the Bible from a statistical standpoint, there is a vast difference in the amount of times fathering, family, sons and daughters versus teaching, preaching, etc. are mentioned. The Bible references family, fathers and similar topics several thousands of times. However, quite the contrast is that only several hundred times is there reference to teaching, preaching and the like. Jesus did equip the disciples to teach and preach, but he taught them to see God as Father. They could then teach and preach from that position. Teaching and preaching is a tool we are all to use in order to help bring the sons and daughters towards their dreams and destiny. It is one tool amongst many. The end goal isn't about people hearing more sermons but whether they were raised up to be Fathers and Mothers themselves who found out their purpose, pursued it and walked in it. We need more Fathers who will get into the lives of the sons and daughters and help them step into their place in life.

For the moment I want to talk about the need to model what fathering looks like from a pulpit standpoint. The goal isn't pulpit ministry for everyone. The goal is every believer walking in the Father's heart towards those around them, bringing the whole earth into the revelation that they are sons and daughters of God. For the last fifteen years, on a wider scale, there has been preaching about fathers and mothers emerging. But we are only still preaching about it. Our walk needs to line up with our talk. We haven't yet seen the model or map of what this can look like practically. Of course, we are all called to model the Father in our every day lives, but a drastic change will take place when we start modeling it from the pulpit. I would also venture to say that it wouldn't hurt us to set the pulpit off to the side and simply sit down as a dad would with his family, and talk to the people that God has entrusted to and around us. This is a core value that I have lived for some time now.

Where are the Fathers?

When getting ready to speak publicly, I try to ask myself, "If this were my own personal family, how would I be communicating and interacting with them? If this were my house, how would I be talking? How would I be worshiping? How would I treat these people if they were my own kids?"

The challenges to answering these questions are that most, if not all of us, have some sort of distorted view of family and of what true fathering really looks like. We are still facing a vast learning curve. When we ask those questions about what would this service look like if this was family, we may not yet have a personal model. Paul says in the King James Version of 1 Corinthians 4:15,

> "For though ye have ten thousand instructors in Christ, yet have ye not many fathers: for in Christ Jesus I have begotten you through the gospel."

In this scripture, Paul is sharing that there are plenty of teachers and instructors sharing the gospel, but he doesn't yet see the fathers.

Who are they?

Where are those who will just sit down and talk life? Where are the Fathers who will break off a piece of their heart and life experiences and share them? Talk to the people like they are hungry for fresh bread. I love preaching and I believe we absolutely need preaching, exhorting, prophetic, teaching etc. But I, also, think that we need to encompass a long lost art - the art of being a dad, publicly.

Keep in mind that I am not after the title of "father." I have had my share of folks call me their father, but the moment I really started to dive into the depths of their heart to start doing some work down there, some have jerked away and said "nope, I don't want you speaking in there." I'm mainly referring to the mindset shift that takes place when you think how a father thinks. For example, what would this be like if I were just being a dad to my kids in the pulpit? Maybe I'd relax a little more. Maybe I would even let my guard down and actually be more real. It's even possible that things might not have to be so polished and perfect.

Church in the Living Room

I believe it is time for us to start asking the question: what would this meeting look like if it were in my living room? There are several different types of living room expressions. One example is when we have a dinner party and have people over to our house and invite them into our living room. We are the hosts and are operating on our best behavior, exhibiting good manners and serving our guests. Then, there is the living room meeting when we are watching our favorite sports team with a group of people that are united with us in support of our team. Now that's a pretty fun experience. (Go 49ers! My favorite football team!) Here we start letting our hair down a bit. But the living room meeting I am talking about is when we invite our closest friends over that we feel comfortable to just be ourselves around. We don't care what we look like around them and they come over sometimes in their pajamas, jeans and t-shirts. We sit around and feel free to let our guards down. We can share our frustrations and our joys, we can laugh and joke around, we can dream and get excited. This last scenario must be transferred over to our church life.

Can you imagine meetings like that? You might be wondering why do we even need to model this in a meeting context? We will never see the reformation in our every day lives until we model the way we are to live in our church settings. It is an interesting dynamic, but people often are only able to step into the atmosphere and anointing of family when it has been modeled publicly for them.

Where Does Family Fit In?

When we talk about family, we need to ask ourselves some questions. Do we want to make family a priority? Haven't we been preaching it for some time? Do we celebrate with understanding those who miss a church service for the sake of a family event?

As we see our culture shifting, people will no longer come to our meetings if we don't understand and affirm them for not being there on any given day. We are not in the same era where it was just the normal routine for people to go to church. We need gathering points and regular times to come together. However, if we are going to see an increase in our influence, we have to shift some of the things we are so set on establishing in order to accommodate what is needed in this present era. We should celebrate the family and those trying to sow into their families and affirm that this is one of the main ministries of every human being.

When many reach the end of their lives you rarely hear them talk about how they wished they could have done more work. Seldom do people look back and have regrets about not doing enough vocational ministry. Most people wish they could have spent more time with their families. When we take vacations or have holidays, we typically spend those breaks with biological family or close friends that have stood the test of time with us. Rarely do we bring people from our staff or church into our holidays or vacations or close and intimate celebrations. What message does that imply?

The desire for family has been imprinted in each of our hearts. Most fathers and mothers ask themselves at the end of a day "Have I done a good job as a parent?" Some don't feel they have done so well and others don't have the tools to truly be successful. I am thankful for the increasing amount of parenting guidance resources available, but I also realize that we need to increase the affirmation of the part of "ministry" that prioritizes our natural family as important.

Jesus himself, when He was dying on the cross, looked at John the beloved and said in John 19:26-27,

> "When Jesus saw his mother there, and the disciple whom he loved standing nearby, he said to his mother, 'Dear woman, here is your son,' and to the disciple, 'Here is your mother.' From that time on, this disciple took her into his home."

He modeled a priority for family.

The No Pressure Zone

Whatever we model, affirm, share, or put out for all to see will be reproduced. We reproduce what we are looking at, valuing and learning from. We share that we value family and marketplace life; but are we creating church life that makes room for family while empowering and affirming them in what they are doing? It's sometimes not the things we say that are communicating, it's what we are not saying. If we say we value family, changing our world and empowering every believer, then our public forums need to reflect that.

I remember when I was in another country with a businessman who had a large prosperous business. He attended church every night to pray and spent many nights in meetings, although that was draining the life out of him. He was being driven out of the culture created from the pulpit that caused him to feel the pressure to attend every service. His schedule was quite full. However, this same man also had a consistent Bible study that he held in his warehouse. He had hungry people from his workplace and other business people who attended these gatherings during the course of their workweek. They were being encouraged and built up. He was doing a great job at creating community within the life of his business. The challenge for him was the pressure that was created from the larger church he was a part of. Whether it was outwardly spoken or he put the pressure on himself, I'm not sure. But he attended many other meetings in the church building, which kept his small amount of extra time constantly tapped. This is not healthy and eventually steals fruit from the places it is needed in.

In essence, you can do all the right things, but if there is still pressure to go to meetings that people may not have time for, then we are not going to get the kind of breakthrough that we desire to see in the marketplace, the seven mountains, and then also in the gathering of a harvest. People only have so much energy and time to give of themselves, and if we are going to be effective in this next era, we must learn to find what God is breathing on and create our responses around that. This follows the pattern of having a flexible wineskin that can continue to grow with the ebbs and flows of life on this earth along with the timings of God.

Tradition Can Stand in the Way

The goal is to create an authentic expression in our meetings that will facilitate and affirm real life events and situations outside of the church context, and determine our functions around that. A pastor friend of mine started a home church a few years ago in a new city.

His plan was to create a new model of family and to do life together with others. They quickly grew to about 30 or so. After several years of doing home church, he noticed that he was having the same issues in the home setting that he used to experience in a traditional church setting. He shared that people came to his home church and would have a great time fellowshipping before the official time the meeting would start. As soon as it came time to start the service, all the genuine fellowship ceased. It became a challenge for him to maintain the life giving exchange throughout the entire service, rather than just before the service. He observed that the mindset always shifted back to: we must be on our best behavior now that church has begun.

I recently experienced a similar situation. I led worship on Christmas Eve and was playing some fun jazzy Christmas songs with my friend on the platform before the official service time began. We were having such a great time goofing around together. We played and sang "Jingle Bells" and "I'm Dreaming of a White Christmas." I sensed a genuine excitement and an increased level of authenticity that created a joyful atmosphere. However, in the back of my mind I knew that at the moment service would officially begin, I would need to lead the people in an official Christmas Eve worship time and that it would be a challenge to bring authentic joy into the room. Why? Because there were a group of folks in attendance that didn't normally attend our church. Family, visiting relatives and folks who were just coming out for a special service. When the "official" meeting began, people would shift from family mode into traditional mode. Joy was not expected in the traditional time nor embraced to the measure that joy could be embraced during the pre-service time.

Let me explain what I mean by traditional mode. Traditional mode is the method and formula that we have acted within for many years. It is a pre-programmed ritual, routine and way of behaving during the service times that we instinctively follow.

The way we engage with God in our services becomes a model by which people engage with God in every day life. If we want to see a shift in what God wants to do in creating genuine family, then we must first model in our meetings what we want to see happen in every day life. God is a Father who has come to raise up sons and daughters. With sons and daughters there is more interchange and interaction. People are more engaged and less passive. Fathers can pick out the voice of a son or daughter in a crowd of voices. They are more in tune with each other's hearts. Well connected sons and daughters can be led with the eyes of a loving, caring father instead of by the rod of a driven schoolmaster.

How are you doing in this regard? How about in times when real correction is needed? Is your love pulled back or drawn off the table?

Let's Get Real

Over the last few years, we have had many prophetic words released about invading the mountains of society and shifting the mind molders of culture. We have also tried new approaches to evangelism through the prophetic, power and releasing the glory. All of those are good, but none of them are bringing the level of evangelism we know in our spirits that we are supposed to see. The seven mountains message and the new and upgraded evangelism approaches will only be effective when we transition out of good performance based meetings into family style identity based meetings. When we begin to transition into a more authentic model to who we are as family in our homes, then we will begin to see our guards come down.

This shift will cause others to bring their guards down and the congregation will begin to relax. The musicians won't have to try so hard for high levels of worship. The preacher won't have to work so hard and won't feel the pressure they always feel. This is a good introduction to the reformation that is needed in the church; to restore a genuine family environment back to the "family" of God. Once we have done that then we will be able to more genuinely live out the same family atmosphere in our work places. Our evangelism will be present and relational evangelism will be experienced with power. Power will flow more authentically in the context of relationships. People won't feel like evangelizing is outside of their normal way of life. The new norm will be walking as a son of God towards brothers and sisters all around us who may not know they belong in our heavenly family yet. As we get comfortable with being family in the corporate church context, then we will be more comfortable modeling family to those all around us that desperately need true connection.

We talk so much about family, when often times our meetings are not congruent with that reality. It is not that our hearts are not leaning towards family; rather it is that our structures aren't. In the next chapter, I will dig deeper into what is coming in the reforming of the local church context so that we can see the harvest we all want to have.

Keith B. Ferrante

Chapter 2

Reforming The Church Service

One of the major shifts we will experience in the next few years is that our meetings will mirror the family message we are preaching. As we see this realized, there will then be an authenticity to what we are speaking to. Authenticity occurs when there is no discrepancy between our actions and words. Your walk matches your talk. Authenticity releases anointing and harvest when you are genuinely living out what you are speaking about.

An Awakening of Authentic Worship

In November of 2013, I headed into a classroom to teach for Dan McCollam's worship school. I had prepared to teach on singing scripture with musical accompaniment. Little did I know that what would happen in that class would mark the beginning of the reformation revealed to me almost fourteen years earlier by the Lord. We'll talk about that specifically at a later point in the book.

I had been very anxious that day leading up to the time I was scheduled to teach. Prior to my class, I was in one of Dano's teaching sessions sitting towards the back of the classroom, when the Holy Spirit began to minister joy to me. That joy helped restore peace and ridded me of anxiety about my teaching time. I was so overwhelmed by the Holy Ghost that I was a small distraction to those towards the back of the class. When the class was dismissed, I stumbled along full of laughter and drunk in the joy of His presence. As I staggered my way towards my teaching session, God spoke to my heart. He said, "The reformation starts now." That thought stayed with me until a later time when I could ponder the magnitude of what He had just declared.

As I entered my classroom, full of joy and the Holy Spirit, one of our supernatural school students approached me. She had a word of knowledge for a hip problem and asked if she could release it. I thought to myself "this doesn't seem to fit the topic I am teaching on." It is strange how sometimes you can wrestle with something like releasing the supernatural, when in fact I love releasing the supernatural. It just seemed to take my mind a few seconds to get wrapped around the idea of releasing a word of knowledge for healing during a music class. After thinking for a few more seconds, I gave her permission to release the word. She released it and sure enough, there was a lady in the class that had the hip problem.

The power of God was electric in the room and as the student prayed, the lady was healed. The classroom had between thirty or forty people who then erupted in praise, joy and celebration of what the Lord had just done. This went on for some time, as spontaneous praise just seemed to go on and on. Other ministry over different individuals went on for some time with power and love being released all around. Eventually we moved into my planned topic for the class, singing scripture to music. The teaching flowed easily out of the presence of God. I began to lead the class through singing Psalm 23. Many were singing at the top of their lungs in a variety of styles with no thought or concern of anyone around them. By the end of that time, the glory of the Lord permeated the room.

As we gathered the class together to hear testimonies of what the Lord had done, the lady who had just been healed shared a testimony. She shared that she had read Psalm 23 for many years to deal with her pain, but this was the first time she had encountered the Lord in Psalm 23 from a healed perspective. She was incredibly touched by that encounter. Another lady in the class shared how the Lord was healing her during our time from some past hurts she had suffered from a divorce. People were publicly being courageously transparent about the deep things of their hearts. The combination of that level of vulnerability, freedom in worship, the spirit flowing through people all in a safe family environment created this reformation moment. After class, people came up to me wanting to continue to pour out the songs they had heard in their spirit during the class time. What vulnerability was being released from the people! What deep things were being shared! What complete and abandoned worship was being released! It was so powerful.

Going Deeper

How did all of this transpire? What was it that created this reform moment? This came from a place where a secure culture was created that allowed exuberant worship, inner healing, and public vulnerability to flow freely. God is after restoring this type of freedom to the body. Creating a safe place for people to encounter Him, receive healing, and allow them to be known at a deeper level. You might say, well I have already had inner healing. He wants to take us much deeper than we presently have experienced. We have barely tapped the surface of the depths of His love and He wants us to corporately and personally step deeper into Him. This will bring more inner healing to us personally and to the body as a whole. It will take a people that courageously create safe havens and spiritual hospitals if we are to see a harvest where people get healed, free, and filled with extravagant public praise.

We create a foundation of safety where people can live authentically real when we ourselves are carrying the acceptance of God in our hearts towards people and their journey towards greater freedom. If we want to see that authenticity released in those that are in need of freedom we must make sure we are modeling what we are proclaiming.

Authenticity as a Lifestyle

Since I have consistently been a part of several churches through itinerant ministry, I have been given the opportunity to know a bit of the character of the individuals that are ministering. A few of the wonderful worship team members that I get to brush shoulders with have so much to offer, but sometimes get caught up in the pressure of trying to release what they have not yet learned to authentically manifest in their own lives. When they try to release something that is not from who they are at the core, lack of transformational power is the result.

Let me give you an example. A couple of the team members at one of these churches tend to be a bit more melancholy in personality and don't exude much joy. They try to engage the congregation in corporate songs of joy when they don't really have much joy in their own personal life. The result is no transformation, no anointing and at times a need to coerce those under their leadership into spiritual activity that has no real authenticity. People can spot when someone's message isn't congruent to their current reality and eventually get turned off by that type of ministry. I have no problem with people's personal journeys to greater freedom and I'm not judging them for having those struggles. I know that we all need grace in areas that we are growing in and personally we each have our own strengths and weaknesses. But the majority of our ministry to others must be released from the places we have true authority in. The lack of authenticity between our message and our lifestyle is seen in the lack of authority that transforms others in that ministry. It becomes evident when we try to lead the congregation in a rejoicing song when it is not currently a part of the fruit we are bearing. You can get away with it for a while but no one wants to continue to be a part of something, which lacks true life.

I know there are times when you are going to bring a sacrifice of joy and choose joy whether you feel it or not. I am fine with that and spent years as a joy impaired worshiper having to learn to release more joy in what I did. It felt awkward and unnatural at first. The point is that when there is a discrepancy in authenticity, you cannot get people to enter into a place that you have little revelation in. If you are normally a very depressed person trying to lead people into joy, it probably isn't going to work so well. If you get people to clap and dance a little to a song that has joy language and even a sound of joy, but it isn't being released through the person with an authentic joy breakthrough, it creates performance in the congregation. Similar to the cartoon Winnie the Pooh characters, Eeyore and Tigger. You can't be like Eeyore, who is known for being depressed, coaxing others to jump for joy like Tigger.

One reason that we have had so little harvest of souls and breakthrough in the desired growth we want to see in our services starts with inauthenticity. People dislike phony people and typically cannot stand dealing with people that are not real.

Performance Pressure

I know we could blame the worshiper for being joyless, but I think the more significant issue at hand is that we have continued to do church and worship the same way. We use different songs and styles but the same low level of vulnerability is present. An authenticity breakthrough is needed. Somewhere along the way, we created pulpits for people to stand behind and worship songs for people to follow, which have contributed to creating a culture where the show must go on. I want to emphasize that I am not campaigning to eliminate church services, worship and preaching. As I have mentioned before, I believe we need all of this. This is not something we should eliminate, but I think we may want to consider trying to find a way to be more congruent to an authentic expression that doesn't propagate performance in those leading.

I have experienced first hand for many years the devastation of what this model has cultivated for so many church leaders – the pressure to have to keep producing a good service week after week. For example, release good worship, prophecy, act joyful, do signs and wonders. Things haven't changed from when we had no signs and wonders, joy and prophecy, to the current time. The same pressure can still be felt in the meetings. I am a third generation pastor and I know the pressure of having to come up with sermons week in and week out, whether you feel like it or not.

We need to ask ourselves, is this family? What did God come to do? Did He come to create meetings or family? Well, we have meetings to work within, so why not create family within them and then maybe we can start having family outside of them.

A Brief Reformation History

Let's look for a brief moment at just a couple of elements that marked the reformation of the 1500's. One thing that marked the times was the inability for the majority of church parishioners to hear the gospel in the language they understood. At the time, the Catholic Church preached the word in Latin, and the majority of the people of the time did not understand a word of it. After quite a struggle, Martin Luther, one of the reformers of that day, wrote the Bible in the language of the people, which was German. This was a revolutionary act and resulted in severe backlash from the Catholic Church. Around that same time, people began publicly hearing the word of God in their own language. That was unheard of then!

That reformation was in some ways about providing access to the gospel Jesus intended it to have. During that time, many people were being coerced to give indulgences (money) to the Catholic Church to ensure that they and their loved ones would have a secure place in heaven. Others could spend months and years never sure if they were really saved, tormented by the thought that they might not make it to heaven. But now through the message of the reformers, getting into heaven became as easy as believing and receiving the good news. Martin Luther received and released the revelation that "The just shall live by faith." That rocked his theology and the theology of the day. We are still being rocked by it. He opened up the reality of the ease by which every person could access heaven. Jesus is the way, and we enter into the way by believing in Him.

Where We Are Today

Now here we are, having lived about five hundred years under that theology. Preaching has been one of the main vehicles to get us where we are today. I love preaching and have been preaching since I was a young boy. In fact, my dad used to let me preach in his pulpit when I was a youth. I have been preaching for over thirty years and love the power of the word released. But I also think we have to ask ourselves what are we looking to as a model for what God is releasing? What does God want to reform? Our preaching has gotten us this far. Let us celebrate that! However, I wonder if it is time to explore some other ways of communicating the gospel so that even more fruit can be realized. I think the fruit we have presently experienced has come from the kind of ministry we have behind the pulpit and from the platform. Much of this fruit has been born because of the reformation that took place hundreds of years ago. We have enjoyed hearing the gospel in our own languages. Praise God for that. But what do people need today? People are crying out for relationship, and they want to see it modeled.

23

I have tried different ways of setting up meetings just to see if I could find something that felt more relaxed, more authentic or even more family-like. One way has been to move the pulpit aside and replace it with a couch where we can model family. At other times I have explored being more fatherly from the pulpit in exchange of a great compelling sermon. I have to ask myself during those times, is He modeling preaching in this season or Fathering? Fathering teaches and preaches, but from a different approach. Both are preaching, but one brings in different fruit than the other. Fathering breaks down fear of punishment, creates safety, and stimulates a culture where others can grow. Preaching can produce great results, but at times leaves us unable to relax and be ourselves. I know that this very message will create stress for preachers, of which I am one. Our identity can be very wrapped up in being a good communicator. But I am wondering if we should hold onto our communication and preaching while asking ourselves could there be another approach for us to learn how to communicate that could produce other fruit needed for this emerging move of God? It is not about a secret new model but rather it's about finding how to move with the ebbs and flows of God in a way that creates a culture where people experience the Father in a family context.

Learning to Relate As A Father

Learning a new communication style can be scary. After 12-15 years of being out of youth ministry, I stepped back into it with fear and trembling. How was I to communicate? What was I to say? How was I to say it? But humbly I stepped into it knowing that God was pleased with me. This freed me so I could explore this different approach, and with that a new boldness came. I found that I had to become more versed with illustrations that worked for a younger crowd. At times I needed to have more fun, but also be passionate and speak as a Father would. I would never have learned these skills had I not been willing to face my fears and step into a new way of communication. The goal is to be able to connect the Spirit of God to the group we are engaging in a relevant and real way.

Growing In New Worship Expressions

In the music arena, I love what God has taught me over the last few years in terms of prophetic song. I enjoyed leading corporate worship for many years. However in the last few years the grace to lead corporate worship was removed from me. God was trying to teach me to step into prophetic song and be comfortable with that as a genuine worship expression. During that time I had a lot of anxiety around this kind of worship and wrestled with thoughts of this not being acceptable in the house of God for me. In the process of developing this song, I noticed that this expression of worship rarely brought on performance anxiety for me. I am so relaxed in this sweet spot and it is a place where I simply hear what God is saying over His children and I sing it over them. I find such great joy in this and have a lot of fun with God.

Now, in this season ask me to lead corporate worship and I can get worked up for days just thinking about it. I led worship for years and still occasionally step into it. But I am provoked to see a more relaxed approach that creates authenticity for those that are leading it. The pressure we put on ourselves and others to create a perfect set of worship to follow can sabotage what God wants to do. God wants us to get real and find a way forward that doesn't create a stage atmosphere or a good entertaining concert. We are a family and should have an increasing measure of family dynamics versus a pressure cooker corporate worship event.

Modeling Authenticity

Whatever we model in our meetings is what we will see expressed in the seven mountains and in our evangelism, which is why we need to shift how our meetings are run. There is still a pressure to perform, to prophesy, to preach a great message, to hit a worship service out of the ballpark, etc. Believe you me, if you are the one leading the worship and you bomb it week after week, others will most likely be finding someone else to fill your shoes very quickly. There is a definite pressure. We have shifted out of what we considered traditional worship and church services years ago. At the time, we thought we were cutting edge, but I tell you there is another edge that must be cut. We must find a way to be real in our midst.

I remember years ago when my wife Heather and I were going down the hill to the church meeting in the morning. She was leading worship and I was preaching. We had one of those mornings where we fought like cats and dogs all the way down. I'm sure none of you have had a morning like that before. We arrived at the church parking lot and she said, "I'm not going in!" In response I said, "Well I'm not going in either." We sat there for a few minutes and then realized if we didn't, then the show wouldn't go on. So we put on our best Sunday behavior, went in and after a few minutes, Heather started leading worship from the piano. I was trying to find some sort of life in me to preach after the arguing we had just been through all the way down the hill. In those circumstances, your spirit isn't ready, you don't want to do anything, and you feel guilty, mad and sad all at the same time.

In the midst of me trying to get ready, and the worship going on for three songs, I heard Heather bang on the piano and stop the worship. She said publicly, "I can't go on." I thought, "Bummer, my cover is blown." She then proceeded to tell the congregation that we weren't doing well in our marriage and that we had a fight that morning. I knew it was over then. Did I want to be real with the church? No. But it was forced on me by my better half; my lovely and courageous wife. We both went and sat down on the front stairs in the church and the people gathered around us and prayed for us, while also feeling a bit sorry for us. There wasn't any preaching that day. The meeting was over. Did I really like that? No. Honestly, I don't like it when people feel sorry for me and don't know how to handle my being real. They want to fix you or tell you they'll be praying for you. Sometimes when you are in that spot, you don't want to be fixed or prayed for. You want to feel like you can have your messy day out there for everyone to see and still retain some dignity as a person. It is humbling to let your stuff hang out there like that.

You might say, "Well brother, God needed to humble you a bit" or "That was good for you." Yes it was, but that way of living life isn't easy, not for the one having to publicly live vulnerably. It's what I'm living for now but have had to fight to want to embrace it.

Getting Off Of The Performance Tread-Wheel

I feel that God wants us to get off our performance-tread-wheel. Whether you are in a trendy church, a revival church, a traditional church, or a home group church, whatever kind of church you are in, it would benefit you to take courage to embrace a new way. I have seen people fall morally who were prophesying at a high level, releasing the anointing, preaching people into tears it was so powerful; yet struggling in private with sin. They lived within a model of ministry that the work of ministry could function while the real life going on behind the scenes was hidden. I am not saying we throw out the baby with the bathwater. I know there is good in every model and there is a need for corporate worship and preaching, etc. But maybe we should just start asking ourselves some questions about our meetings.

First, you may want to ask yourself, are your meetings producing the kind of fruit that you want to see produced? We want to see different fruit, but we are not creating what will bring the kind of fruit we want. Do we want to see the harvest come through our doors? We are not going to see them come through our doors while we manifest inauthentic worship. The spirit realm perceives a lack of truth and capitalizes on it. The enemy waits until we are beginning to build momentum and then he pulls the plug on those who have been leading the charge, but have unaddressed sin, hiddenness or inauthenticity. I believe that if we continue down this road, it will be more and more costly if we don't change the way we move forward.

The seven sons of Sceva had to learn a lesson about authenticity the hard way and we need to learn the same lesson from them so we don't let the enemy tear us apart as he did them. Acts 19:13-17 demonstrates this,

> "Some Jews who went around driving out evil spirits tried to invoke the name of the Lord Jesus over those who were demon-possessed. They would say, 'In the name of Jesus, whom Paul preaches, I command you to come out.' Seven sons of Sceva, a Jewish chief priest, were doing this. [One day] the evil spirit answered them, 'Jesus I know, and I know about Paul, but who are you?' Then the man who had the evil spirit jumped on them and overpowered them all. He gave them such a beating that they ran out of the house naked and bleeding. When this became known to the Jews and Greeks living in Ephesus, they

were all seized with fear, and the name of the Lord Jesus was held in high honor."

What was the deal? They weren't carrying authentic power themselves. They were trying to operate in Paul's grace, since they didn't have a genuine encounter of their own with Jesus to operate from. The devil perceived it and took advantage of them, beating them up. We can't let that happen to us.

Live Authentically Powerful

We must find a way to create a culture where the people that are leading the meetings can be real, let their guards down and be family. I'm talking about the kind of family dynamics when you are at home with your spouse and children and no one else is around. When you walk around the house in your skivvies. When people see you with your messed up hair and bad morning breath. Are we ready to see each other that way? When we get to the place where we can live as that kind of family in our meetings, we will see an unprecedented harvest of souls coming through our doors and lives. When we learn to live authentically with nothing hidden, we will be so attractive to people.

I love a quote from Eddie Murphy's character in the movie Daddy Day Care. He said, "Why don't you stop trying to cram so much head knowledge down their throats and just talk to them?" (In reference to him speaking to the teacher at a strict, performance-driven daycare school.) Why do we always have to feel the pressure to preach and to communicate something wonderful? Or feel the constant need to hit a home run? Why don't we just relax, be a bit more vulnerable and sit down and try something more family oriented, more relevant? Maybe we could interview some believers that are doing life in the marketplace. Maybe we could just loosen up a bit ourselves and share from our hearts those things that have brought breakthrough for us.

The world wants real. They want real people with real answers. They want people that will not judge them but will love them. They will happily get out of their sin and mess when they feel like we genuinely see their mess and still love them through it. How can we help them out of their messes and harvest them when we have so many messes of our own that we aren't willing to deal with? How are we going to see a harvest when we aren't willing to allow any messes to take place in our meetings? I have seen the pressure over and over again in so many places; including good places and even fiery glory places. There is this pressure to have another good meeting where everything flows well and looks good.

I know good worship too. I can get worked up like the best of them over a bad worship set, or an inexperienced worship leader. I can get critical and start throwing grumbly bombs of accusation into the atmosphere when the announcements last too long and the sermon is more boring than a college lecture on English. (Nothing against English, but it was not my cup of tea.) But I have been learning to take down my guard. This is not supposed to be a performance; this is not supposed to be a platform. I know that this is the way it has been done for many, many years. The pulpits used to be high and lofty. Many of them have come down to more ground level literally, but I think we may need to shift some of those pulpits to a sofa or love seat for a while and just sit and have some low-key unplugged worship. The goal isn't a different look, or a different building structure; the goal is creating an opportunity where life can be experienced on a more real level.

Authenticity To Increase Anointing

In a recent season the youth group needed me to be much more involved on a weekly basis. I canceled my traveling schedule and chose to be at home in this season. I was provoked. I didn't want to continue to create a culture where we had a full band and a completely loaded sound system with a small amount of presence. I noticed that every time I had the youth band lead worship off the sound system, there was a dramatic increase in the anointing. Eventually, I led worship for a few weeks to model what I felt that God was releasing. It was a bit of a struggle for me, as I prepared to lead the youth in worship. I wondered if it would "work." I decided that I wasn't going to lead any prepared songs, but that instead I would just release the Father's heart prophetically over them and just be who I am in my private times with Jesus.

I led worship like this for a couple of weeks, and it didn't seem to get much of a response. Then, I asked the youth band, who are great musicians and have a lot of anointing, how they felt about the worship. I asked them what their favorite worship times had been over the previous few years and one talented young man said the last two weeks had been. I responded in disbelief asking "How come?" His response was because of the prophetic and spontaneous worship. I couldn't believe it. It wasn't miked, it was low-key, it was nothing fancy or extravagant; but yet it was authentic to me. These talented young men wanted to follow my lead and take the opportunity in the following weeks to lead worship as I had from the couches. Now couch led worship isn't the hot ticket but authentic worship is. They needed to take a bit of time to find worship outside of performance. For them electric and loud could be authentic, but for that season they needed to explore something more casual. They needed something that allowed the pressure to perform to fall off so they could find their authentic sweet spot.

31

We started taking steps to bring the atmosphere of our youth meetings down from the full band set up with the flashy lights, curtains and high energy stimulation to couches, low-key and more of a living room feel. They actually wanted that. Every time we entered worship from that place, we started to feel more and more of His presence. The level of breakthrough we had been experiencing with our youth opened up in worship. The youth have regularly had encounters with God; they have let their own guards down, and have been more open and coming forth. The change in the atmosphere has been a direct result of us working together to create a more authentic culture. We started to just sit down during the meetings and talk with the youth about life. There is a safety that has been created there that is bearing fruit.

As time progressed it has been great seeing the youth step back into their normal electric sound with the full band and finding that a new pressure free worship has begun to emerge there as well. The presence has been much stronger. The authentic worship seemed to have so much more life on it after a season of letting go of the big sets. The key isn't loud music, soft couches, pulpits, house settings or church buildings, but really it is finding a place where you and others can be genuine together. Where is the place that you allow people to see you as a real person? Where is the place that you engage people as you would your own closest and most personal family?

Greater Breakthroughs

If we are going to see a breakthrough in different kinds of fruit, such as the fruit of authenticity, we have to be authentic and genuine. When we are real and true to who we are publicly and privately, we will begin to create a culture in which people get free. We so desperately need this in the body of Christ.

In the next chapter, I will talk about how to create a personal culture where you are truly authentically vulnerable. Vulnerability is the fruit of living in the light. When we learn to live in the light, we will have an endless stream of people coming and giving their lives to Jesus.

Keith B. Ferrante

Chapter 3

Reformation Motto:
The Just Shall Live By Real

A round the year 2000, I asked the Lord what the next reformation was going to be about. I thought to myself that there is a major reformation in the church every five hundred years. This must be the time for another one. As I began to press in to discover what this reformation would be about, God spoke to me. He shared a phrase with me that at the time almost didn't sound like a proper sentence. He said six words, "The Just shall live by real." Though it didn't make much sense then, I knew it was a phrase that would stay with me for years.

As time went on, that statement has increasingly resonated with me. I know it truly is a foundational slogan for those who want to enter into another dimension in God. Let me explain what this means to me. Those who know they are accepted, forgiven, loved and walking in God's grace will begin to live real and authentic lives that are completely in the light. People are so attracted to this, that when we finally see this happen, it will cause an unprecedented harvest. It is a real place, a place where God's glory will not be hindered in us. This is a place where people will see Christ shining through us. He is the desire of the nations. When they see Him in us because we are now living fully in the light, we will have all the influence we can handle. We will then draw a people to Him who will help reform the culture that we live in to reflect the heaven that they have met in us.

But how do we actually live in the light?

Heaven Revealed

We have to see what is going on around the throne and in God. What is the atmosphere of heaven? There are many different things going on in heaven, but what brings us to this place is found in Revelations 4:6, "before the throne there was what looked like a sea of glass, clear as crystal."

There is a sea of glass around the throne room. Nothing is hidden in heaven. Everything is seen. According to Ephesians 2:6, we are seated in heavenly places with Christ right now. And God raised us up with Christ and seated us with him in the heavenly realms in Christ Jesus.

As we begin to realize in our spirit man that we are seated in heavenly places and what is going on in heaven, we will begin to reflect that reality. Our goal is to bring to earth what is in heaven. The Lord taught us to pray that way in Matthew 6:10 when he said,

"Your kingdom come,
Your will be done
on earth as it is in heaven."

We need to learn to see what is in heaven, where the scriptures say we are actually seated. As we see that reality, we can then pray for it to come here. Our hearts will then begin to manifest that reality through our lives. The goal is clear. Living real, nothing hidden, completely in the light, as He is light. When we learn how to live completely real and in the light, hiding nothing; whether it be good, bad or ugly, we will begin to see the light of Christ shine through us like never before.

Let Your Light Shine

I used to wonder what it meant to shine your light for Jesus. We grew up singing songs about shining your light and were encouraged to lead people to Jesus. One day, it became a bit clearer to me. Matthew 5:16 says, "In the same way, let your light shine before men, that they may see your good deeds and praise your Father in heaven." Our father is the Father of lights. We are the children of light. The fruit of light is found in Ephesians 5:8-9,

> "For you were once darkness, but now you are light in the Lord. Live as children of light (for the fruit of the light consists in all goodness, righteousness and truth."

One of the fruits of light is truth, which means "nothing hidden." When we create a culture where we are no longer hiding, but have found how to truly live in the light, then people will be drawn to that light and will want that light for themselves. Wherever Jesus was on earth, He had an endless stream of broken and hurting people hunting Him down because they saw the genuine light and truth in Him. That light is now in us.

John 1:9 says, "The true light that gives light to every man was coming into the world." Jesus is the true light and in verse 14, it further says about Jesus, "The Word became flesh and made his dwelling among us. We have seen his glory, the glory of the One and only, who came from the Father, full of grace and truth." He is the light and the truth. Both light and truth reveal complete purity, honesty, authenticity and love. Jesus was the same on the outside and the inside. He was real, good and truthful. He wants to reveal that side of Himself to us so that we can manifest that same light in our lives.

Acceptance Comes as You Live in the Light

Those who know they are accepted and loved completely will live real and in the light. The light is extremely contagious. I have spent the last 15 years being shown the unconditional acceptance of the heavenly Father through a variety of earthly mothers, fathers, sisters and brothers. I have also heard more times than I can count from the heavenly Father Himself how much He absolutely loves, accepts and is proud of me. As I began to believe that was actually true, I began to let more of my hidden thoughts, struggles, wrong agendas and challenges out in the light to be seen by safe fathers, mothers and brothers in the Lord. As I allowed those areas to be brought into the light, I was able to identify the people that were safe for me to reveal a life of truth. I learned that I could have a terrible day, fall and get in the mud of life around many of the fathers and mothers that God gave me. Not only did they accept me, but cleaned the dirt off me, helped me get washed in who God said I was and caused me to see myself more closely aligned with how my heavenly Father sees me. This created a purity that exudes out of me.

Love and acceptance flows out of me because of the freedom I gained in living open and in the light. I am certainly still growing in this, but I do have a lot of grace for people's messes. I know that everyone has messes and we need people in our lives that can love us in our messes and help us out of them. As I have become more secure in the fact that I don't have to hide anything in the company of my friends and fathers, I have gained an authority in the spirit realm. The devil can come to me, but he has nothing in me. I am not saying that I don't have any issues to deal with, or character development to work through; it just means that people who care about me and carry the Father's heart for me are already aware of all that. The devil can try to say, "I'm going to publicly shame you

Keith for that thought you've been wrestling with." I can tell him, "Well you could try if you wanted, but all that is already out in the light and being taken care of." The people around me are helping me break through in those areas of growth. So I can say with confidence, "I'm not going to listen to you any longer devil." He is the accuser and the Lord shut his mouth through the cross. Colossians 1:22-23 illustrates this,

> "But now he has reconciled you by Christ's physical body through death to present you holy in his sight, without blemish and free from accusation if you continue in your faith, established and firm, not moved from the hope held out in the gospel."

When we learn to live real and in the light, we will begin to attract people to us that want to be fully known. I have found more and more people that feel compelled to share with me the things that they have struggled through, since they feel safe to share. I exude the same love that was given to me. It doesn't mean I don't struggle at times with frustration with people for continuing to repeat the same unhealthy patterns in their lives, but I really work at being caring, compassionate, and patient with people. I know that is the way to freedom. When we accept people where they are at, including their messes, we can help them step into freedom for themselves. In turn, they will desire to hang out with us since they feel safe with us.

Let's Get Vulnerable

Creating a safe culture in our meetings and in our personal lives is an important fruit to cultivate if we want to see a sustainable harvest of people that are truly obtaining freedom. When I caught a revelation of this way of living, I immediately tried to introduce it to my church and leadership team. I spent three years telling my leaders all of the struggles I was going through, my feelings and issues. They spent the next bit of time trying to fix me, which just made me more upset. I didn't realize what was going on. The unwanted fixing would hurt me, but then I would just continue to give them more information.

One of my mentors said to me, "Keith, the problem is that you are metaphorically jumping into the swimming pool without any clothes on, and everyone else is watching you while sitting around the edges of the pool fully clothed. What you need to do is take off your socks, get in the pool and wait there until they take their socks off and join you. Then, you can proceed to take other layers of clothes off as they do." In other words, vulnerable and genuine relationships have to be developed in stages, both privately and publicly. We are not ready as a corporate body to handle a fully authentic experience. We have to slowly progress towards vulnerability as a way of life. We aren't ready to jump right in yet with only our birthday suits on initially; it must be the result of a progression through relationship.

I also learned that if you share vulnerable situations from the pulpit that you have not already worked out or dealt with in your own life, you could experience shame. As a feeler of spiritual things, I can feel shame hit me in my physical eyes when I have shared something vulnerable that is in the wrong setting or context. As an outward or verbal processor, I have had to learn where and with whom I could be vulnerable with. Not everyone is able to handle and accept me without feeling the need to fix me when I have not invited him or her into that process.

When we share something vulnerable, we are giving a piece of our inner self to that person. It's like a precious pearl discovered in the deep ocean. The course of action that the other person or audience does with that pearl determines whether they get another pearl or not. I have learned how to create vulnerable cultures where others can also begin to get real themselves, let down their hair and let their heart out. It is a wonderful culture to create because it is where true freedom happens.

I once led a men's group that helped me get my first win in this area of creating an authentic culture. We went through the book "Wild at Heart" by John Eldridge. It was a great book, and we went through the workbook that asked some great questions, which led to some vulnerable discussions. As I have mentioned before, the goal of the reformation that is upon us is to create public and private venues for people to live authentically. Creating that type of culture among men can be difficult. I had to set the stage weekly with the men and remind them that we were not here to help, fix, give advice, or even pray for each other. We were simply going to listen to each other and practice the art of caring for someone else. There is the time and place for prayer, advice, and help; but this was not that time.

Every week we had someone speak something vulnerable and every week someone would try to fix that person and give him a good scripture or advice from their own personal life to help their struggling brother. Every time that would happen, I would have to interrupt the advice giver and say, "Stop!" This is not the time to fix one another but rather this is the time to protect each other's hearts, create a safe place where we can simply share our hearts without imposing advice or scripture upon each other. After some weeks, we finally reached a safe culture. When we finally did, we had men that had never shared open up and share deep things that you would have never imagined they had been through. Some of these things tore our hearts up. The men that had rarely publicly cried began to cry and pour out their deep places and I knew that we had discovered the pot of gold at the end of the rainbow. Eureka! We had discovered a place where vulnerability could be realized.

Creating a Culture of Breakthrough

The culture of safety and authenticity is where breakthrough happens. In this atmosphere, freedom is the result. It is a good start to confess a sin issue or struggle in front of someone at the altar, but it is another level entirely when you are able to open your heart up to others on a consistent basis, as in the men's group. Taking that up another level is when you learn how to create a culture in your personal life and invite both men and women in whom you can trust with the deep recesses of your soul.

Unfortunately, much of my upbringing and the church culture I experienced around me created hiddenness rather than openness. When peoples' sins came out, they would be shunned from ministering or sent away for several years of rehabilitation. Now I know that rehab is a good thing. But instead of helping people obtain freedom, this actually contributed to an increase in hiddenness. This in turn caused sin to maintain a foothold growing into a stronghold. Whenever there isn't a safe place for people to get their sins out because of fear of what people will say or think, or for fear of punishment; then sin will hide and eventually destroy. It's like a cancer that can grow out of control if not exposed and eradicated. We must learn to create a culture that builds safety into every level if we are going to see the kind of freedom that will bring true transformation.

In the next chapter, I will share the process needed to move from being in bondage, to getting issues of vulnerability out in the open, resulting in much needed personal freedom.

Chapter 4

The Path To Reform

The reformation that is upon us needs to reshape the church so that pre-Christians will have an easier way into the fold. This will then allow them to access a true place of freedom in God. The reason we haven't yet had the kind of harvest desired is because there isn't a culture in the church that is distinctively unique from the culture outside the church. Now some might argue that they have a successful and large church with many new converts. I might respond with, "I'm glad that you are seeing fruit in one area, but what kind of fruit are you bearing in transformation? Are you bearing the fruit of light and truth, or bearing the fruit of hiddenness and performance? You may be bearing the fruit of salvations, but what about transformations?" Both salvation and transformation are absolutely essential to the body of Christ. However, salvation requires one culture and transformation requires another.

Culture of Vulnerability

Our churches are filled with people who profess the name of Jesus, but whose lives can be shrouded with darkness, sin and shame. I'm not necessarily referring to the sin that leads to death and destruction. But rather, I'm referring to the many little sins and hindrances that are still internally destructive if there isn't a culture of safety to bring those issues out into the light. I've been around the church long enough to know that many people haven't learned how to create a culture in their lives that invites continual vulnerability and light. Thankfully I have been around fathers in the faith, who have been a safe place for the deep places of my heart to be exposed and have allowed the hurt that dwells there to be seen. I have also had some of them show me how to access those deep places and have led the way in encouraging me that there is a way to continually live in the light.

It has broken my heart to watch people perform in ministry for years and then suddenly have a big disaster come forth, which exposes their lifestyle of sin to the public. It doesn't have to be this way. It's not God's heart that sin is dealt with in this manner. This is the devastating affect of not creating a culture within our churches that is safe. Instead, much of our culture creates great public performance while the private life is hidden for a time. Sadly, sins grow to the point where they are publicly uncovered and then shouted aloud from the rooftops for many to scoff at and accuse the church of being a hypocrite. This could easily be avoided if we only had the courage to create a different way to freedom, a biblical way to openness. A culture where the Father is present in everything we do.

Representing The Father

We are to represent the Father or re-present the Father to everyone around us. We are His sons, which means that we have the DNA of Dad in us. Whether I am a friend, a father or a son to someone, I can still represent the Father's heart to him or her. Jesus was the Son of God and perfectly represented the Father in every way. Jesus tells His disciples in John 14:9,

> "Don't you know me, Philip, even after I have been among you such a long time? Anyone who has seen me has seen the Father. How can you say, 'Show us the Father'?"

Each of us is to represent the Father in order to create a fatherly environment in manifesting His character. I don't need to be called your father to represent the Father to you. It's not about titles. It's about love. True fathers in the faith carry such a place of acceptance in them that allows those around them to feel safe. This helps those around them to grow in living a lifestyle in the light and freedom from hiddenness.

Embrace Your Process

At times, I have observed the challenge of certain people that struggle with process, or going through a process; particularly in cultures where the grace message is strongly advocated. I am a strong believer in the grace of God. I know it is by His power that I have found my way into heaven. But I do believe that if I want to walk in the sensitivity of heaven, there are some things that I have to consistently and repeatedly deal with that might not immediately leave me through one act of believing.

In recent years I went through a season of discovering the joys that sanctification itself wasn't a process, but happened at the beginning through accepting Jesus as Lord. Hebrews 10:10 was a pillar for me in this,

> "And by that will, we have been made holy (Sanctified) through the sacrifice of the body of Jesus Christ once for all."

I have been co-crucified, co-buried, co-resurrected and co-seated with Christ. This means that the work internally has been done through Jesus. My confession of the revelation of what He did causes me to have access to the treasures of His victory. I have been given every bit of His power to live successfully, but there still is a process that we have to go through to manifest the freedom He freely gave. Over the last months, I have had to wrestle through what repentance means in light of the fact that the work has been finished in me already. It seemed so opposite of what I had just fought so hard to get a revelation of. The revelation was that Christ is in me and because of that I am a new creation; totally pure, innocent, accepted and right before God. All of that is so true, but I have learned that there are many people who believe this teaching on an intellectual level alone and not experientially. They are shrouded in darkness and shame, allowing internal lies that have become strongholds to control them. They know the grace message, but are unable to stay free in areas where the enemy has tempted them. This could be with sexual sin, the lust of the eyes, anger, lack of love, bitterness issues, or a variety of other areas. There is a process that you have to go through in order to get out of these inferior ways and create a stronghold of Christ in you so that you truly do walk in the fruit of the Spirit.

So what is the process we have to be ready to walk through and learn to walk others through if we are going to reform the culture we are in? Here is a preview of the context to come. First you have to start by repenting as you get a revelation of the fear of the Lord and His Kingship over your life. Second, you need to recognize His incredible mercy and out of that confess to the Lord all areas that need cleansing and freedom. Third, you must confess before the right people and accept the process of development needed to create and cultivate a different environment in you. Finally, you have to demonstrate the fruit of repentance to truly be free. Each of these keys needs to be navigated in the context of loving and caring Fathers and Mothers in the faith.

Journey Towards A Life Of Freedom

So let's talk about the first step towards a life of freedom. First, we have to get a revelation that Jesus is Lord and King of our lives.

How do we get a heart-felt revelation that He is Lord of our lives? We have to first see Him in His goodness, mercy, and love towards us. That while we were sinners, He died for us. Next, we have to get so overwhelmed with the fact that He bought us and we are not our own. In the bible, we can observe that the people who walked with God throughout their entire lives, never giving up their faith, were the same people who had encountered Jesus in His glory. The same applies today as well. Paul saw the light of Christ and it blinded him. It also caused him to fear the Lord and become His servant. He endured many persecutions and much suffering because he had been transformed in the overwhelming glory of Christ that he had experience firsthand. It was the fear of the Lord that allowed Paul to stay the course throughout his life. We can't expect people to come to a place of fearing the Lord if they have not yet encountered His love. Romans 2:4 says, "Or do you show contempt for the riches of his kindness, tolerance and patience, not realizing that God's kindness leads you toward repentance?"

The times I have experienced freedom from sinful thoughts trying to lead me into sinful actions was when His love captured me. Sometimes it was His voice speaking to me as a Father that convicted me and reminded me of His goodness and mercy. He is a jealous husband that wants a bride totally for Himself. He is not going to share us with other affections. When we see His power and encounter His goodness, then we have to choose to yield fully to Him. Hebrews 11 refers to those who followed the Lord through many difficulties because they had encountered the invisible one. Encountering Him caused them to follow Him through highs and lows because they knew He was faithful. Moses saw Him and it drove the fear of the Lord into his heart, which kept him from sinning. Hebrews 11:25-26 says,

"He chose to be mistreated along with the people of God

rather than to enjoy the pleasures of sin for a short time. He regarded disgrace for the sake of Christ as of greater value than the treasures of Egypt, because he was looking ahead to his reward."

Revelation of the King Leads to Fruitfulness

Out of truly seeing Him, we will reform our lives to reflect the fullness of Him. One of the indicators that we are getting a revelation of Him as King is that we begin to bear the fruits of His Spirit. God wants us to walk in the fruit of His Spirit. Many have talked about it and preached on it; but we haven't yet seen the fullness of these fruits manifested in a body of believers. When the fullness of love, joy, peace, patience, kindness, goodness, gentleness, faithfulness, and self-control are manifested through us, we will be so contagious that people will desire so desperately what we have. We have seen a few individuals walk in some of these, but to see the body fully manifesting the fruits of God's Spirit will bring in a harvest, guaranteed. These fruits are the high water mark of a successful Christian. They cannot be earned because they have been freely given to us, but yet, there is a process we have to go through to see them manifest in us to the measure that God manifests them in Himself.

The fruit of self-control is a great marker for us to tether our hearts around through the leading of the Spirit of God. How do you know something is of God versus something is of the devil? By it's fruit. The devil advocates everything that is impure, dark, and provides instant gratification, but fails to reveal the long-term torment following. Our cultures have been saturated with darkness and the answer to getting free is the restoration of the fear of the Lord. The fear of the Lord is realized when we begin to recognize that Jesus is still King. We must remember that nothing He has commanded has changed, despite laws that have changed in our legal system that declare certain sins to be legal. Whether the governmental laws of our nations declare sin is legal, accessible, and available doesn't mean that it won't have dire consequences should we embrace and engage in that sin. Also, even if the church declares that certain sins are acceptable, this doesn't take away from the delusions that will infiltrate those who embrace them. Romans 6:23 says, "For the wages of sin is death, but the gift of God is eternal life in Christ Jesus our Lord."

That was true when it was written and is still true today. Sin still leads to death. Walking in the freedom that we have in Christ still produces life. We have freedom from sin, not freedom to sin. It would highly benefit us to get so saturated in our spirits with the fact that Jesus is still King. His laws never changed despite the fact that He died and rose again and gave us the ability to choose life.

The Truth About Grace

Some people feel like grace came to give them the ability to do whatever they want to do, but Titus 2:11-12 says,

> "For the grace of God that brings salvation has appeared to all men. It teaches us to say 'No!' to ungodliness and worldly passions, and to live self-controlled, upright and godly lives in this present age..."

A true grace message will never leave us in sin, but will set us free from sin. The wonderful gift of God has freed us from sin. Anytime we agree with the legal system around us and enter into a sin that is considered legal from a governmental perspective, church perspective, or even personal perspective, we are still welcoming death into our midst. Abraham Lincoln said, "No law can give me the right to do what is wrong." The torment of darkness is not enjoyable for anybody and produces nothing but death and destruction despite its acceptability or legality. In my home country, homosexual marriages are becoming more and more legal, pornography is a screen touch away, countless babies are murdered through abortion and smoking marijuana, a gateway drug into deeper drugs, is a doctor's order away. Jesus the King set up a moral code for us, and inviting sinful things into our bodies and spirits will cause us devastation. These sins will wreak havoc in our lives and families. Jesus still loves you when you choose sin, but sin always leads to death. It isn't Jesus releasing death over you, but rather it is sin that opens the door to the demonic realm in your life.

Briefly look at the sin of offense and observe the devastating consequences of choosing to agree with the enemy. Matthew 18 tells us that if you have an offense against your brother, you are inviting the demonic tormentors into your life. KJV. Matthew 18:33-34,

> "Shouldest not thou also have had compassion on thy fellow servant, even as I had pity on thee? And his lord was wroth, and delivered him to the tormentors, till he should pay all that was due unto him."

You certainly can have offense in your life if you want. You certainly can choose to be bound up by it; but the anguish of offense is ultimately not worth it.

True Freedom

When we are truly caring for what the Master cares about, we will not want anything to do with choices that invite the spirit of death. True freedom in life can only be found in the context of

Jesus as Lord and master. He is still King, and freedom biblically was established within the confines of Lordship. 2 Corinthians 3:17 says it like this. "Now the Lord is the Spirit, and where the Spirit of the Lord is, there is freedom."

There is true freedom where He is the Lord and has been welcomed as Lord. This is part of the culture that He is reforming us to. How do we have a true culture of people that are free of sin and filled with glory? We first must have people that carry the Father's heart and want to protect what God desires. We must be known as people that accept others in the midst of their sin and shame because God is merciful with those in sin. We must also hold the place in our hearts that God did not come to keep you in your sin, but to free you from it. It doesn't matter how it's presented. Sin really does destroy. The devil is a professional liar. He tried to make sin look accepting, lovely and even OK; but in the end, sin does nothing but destroy and devastate. Take for example someone believing the lie that having an affair will be so fulfilling to his or her unmet needs. Is that ever true? No, there is destruction, pain, and hurt to all involved. It can take years for the wounds from that sin to fully heal.

We need Fathers and Mothers that can speak into others' lives that are in the midst of such sin and help them climb out of it. In order to do that, Fathers must help those in sin recognize that their behavior will devastate them. However in the same heartbeat they can say I love you and I am committed to walking with you out of this.

Repent

This brings us to the next part of reformation, which is repentance. In order to truly get free, you need to confess your sins.

I know this might seem so basic, but it is really profound to me in light of the fact that Jesus' grace still has a process involved in it. Confession is actually a stimulant of receiving the grace of God in our lives. When we acknowledge that He is King of our lives, He will shine the light on areas He wants us to eliminate.

We must grab ahold of the revelation that a single act of disobedience, or even living in rebelliousness as a lifestyle (intentionally or not) really can damage our intimacy with God. He always loves us no matter what, but sin does separate and can cause us to hide in shame from God as well as other people. Adam and Eve's first response to an act of disobedience was to hide in shame from the one who loved them. God didn't stay away, but rather came seeking them. I don't believe the lie that your sins separate God from you, but rather they separate you from the awareness of God. They invite confusion, destruction, torment, shame, disgrace, and a host of other problems from the demonic realm. Sin devastates us, but first slowly desensitizes us. Ephesians 4:17-19 says it like this,

> "So I tell you this, and insist on it in the Lord, that you must no longer live as the Gentiles do, in the futility of their thinking. They are darkened in their understanding and separated from the life of God because of the ignorance that is in them due to the hardening of their hearts. Having lost all sensitivity, they have given themselves over to sensuality so as to indulge in every kind of impurity, with a continual lust for more."

Sin results in a downward spiral away from relationship with God and decreased sensitivity to the Holy Spirit, and eventually ends up in full-blown impurity with a desire for more. We must not dare believe the lie that grace covers sin. Grace doesn't cover sin, grace frees from sin. The consequence of sin is death. The benefit of embracing Christ and His fruit is life. I choose life. I realize that temptations of the world, propagated by media and culture, have been pushed at us from so many electronic devices and have not served us well. Personally, when I have fasted from television, electronics, and certain conversations with people, I have noticed an increase in my sensitivity to God. I have also experienced an increased awareness in areas of my life that had been previously and subtly desensitized. We can easily get numbed over a long and slow process of wearing down our walls of resistance until we allow things in that we never would have before.

I am amazed at how many filthy movies people allow into their minds and then wonder why they struggle so much with the issues they struggle with. There is always a cost for allowing certain things in through your eye-gates. Compromise filters into your spirit, creating a stronghold of agreement inside of you and then comes out of you through actions that later eventually destroy you. I encourage you to try an experiment of this for yourself. Take a fast from something that you watch on TV, or that you view on the Internet. I guarantee that you will notice a vast increase in sensitivity to the Holy Spirit. It is like fasting sugar for a month. When you consume sugar again after the fast, you instantly notice how overly sweet the simplest foods are. Barbeque sauce or even ketchup may seem too sweet after a sugar fast. Your senses have been heightened. You feel so much better when you have much less sugar in your body, but after awhile of going off the fast, you can slide back into the same old patterns of massive sugar intake. Your body becomes desensitized again. This is an illustration of the same process that the media can use to desensitize us to the Holy Spirit. We don't even realize that we are opening little gates of hell into many areas of our lives and inviting little tormentors in to harass us. They don't take us out immediately, but they steal our joy, health, peace, intimacy with God, and so many other benefits of the kingdom are lost. In the end, they aren't so little, but have become massive conduits of destruction, pain, shame and loss of life.

Confession of The King

When we get a revelation that the pure light-filled King of Glory wants to be with us, and that sin, shame, compromise and hiddenness have separated us from that reality in our lives; there must be a confession before Him. Our confession should come from genuine revelation of His purity, His light, His goodness and His love. Our hearts need to cry out, "Oh God, please forgive me for letting corrupt things into my spirit. It is not desirable compared to your greatness. It is junk food compared to the healthy intake of daily heavenly manna, and I don't want that filth filling my spirit any more. I want the sense of your presence in my life and the awareness of you all the time."

Samson's Compromises Cost Him

I don't want to be like Samson who carried the anointing while walking in a lifestyle of compromise and sin. He continued to release God's power while getting in bed with a prostitute. He didn't even recognize when the power had finally left him. Judges 16:20-21,

> "Then she called, 'Samson, the Philistines are upon you!' He awoke from his sleep and thought, 'I'll go out as before and shake myself free.' But he did not know that the Lord had left him. Then, the Philistines seized him, gouged out his eyes and took him down to Gaza. Binding him with bronze shackles, they set him to grinding in the prison."

It was a sad and painful awakening that finally opened Samson's eyes to the blindness he finally experienced in the end. It was the subtle little compromises that weren't dealt with over an extended period of time that sedated Samson long before the final seduction took out his eyes and his anointing. Even then, the goodness of God was so gracious that there was hope for Samson. The Lord met him at the end of his life one more time, but the devastation of departing from God's character was very costly. We have to recognize and let our hearts be gripped with a true confession before God that changes us. I remember the Lord convicting me when I was about to look at something impure on television. He said, "Keith, you know when you look at that, you don't just hurt your wife, but you hurt me." Ouch! That cut to a deep place of my heart. Every time He does that, I am so thankful for His patience and His revelation that frees me from damaging my connection with Him.

Confession: True Repentance

The third principle is to confess before others in order to bring about true repentance. It may sound a bit shocking to hear, but confession before God alone rarely creates sustainable freedom. I remember many times when I declared before the Lord that I would never do that thing again, look at that, or say that. Whatever I struggled with never actually left me until I brought it out into the light before others. I began to stay free when I confessed before trusting mothers, fathers or friends that carried a dad's heart for me.

A culture must be created that people feel safe in and want to confess to us. I know that I am in a secure culture because I have had many safe fathers helping me grow in purity and Kingdom character. I exude and extend that same grace to others. Safety causes an opening in the heavens, which causes people to want to open up and confess their sins, shames and vulnerable areas of their lives. They feel a conviction about their issues and know that I am a safe place for them to get free. You may want to ask yourself what your typical initial reaction is when people share these kinds of private issues with you. Is your response filled with judgment, or condemning biblical knowledge of how they missed the mark? Or rather is it full of acceptance, care, love and wisdom? Your response will either attract many more to you or repel them away from you. Rarely are people able to truly manifest the character of acceptance and grace towards others if they haven't had others demonstrate a safe environment for them.

A place of true freedom can be experienced when there is confession before people. There is no way around this truth. James 5:16 says it this way,

> "Therefore confess your sins to each other and pray for each other so that you may be healed. The prayer of a righteous man is powerful and effective."

This kind of culture is so wonderful to create, but can be scary and intimidating at first. In this culture, people can truly let their sins and faults out in front of safe carriers of the Father's heart, and in that context healing will result. There are many wonderful ministries around that release inner healing; deliverance, sozo, counseling, 12 step programs, etc. All of these programs are fantastic and needed for the body of Christ. However, sustainable freedom can only be created and maintained when you learn how to develop trusting relationships around you in which you can confess your sins, faults, and challenges as well as lying thoughts swirling in your head.

Many people can obtain freedom initially after a counseling session, or as long as they are in a program of accountability. But often they are not able to stay free because they haven't learned how to find and invite in the right people that will help them to maintain freedom. If we are to continue to be free, we need safe Fathers regularly speaking into us and we must have the courage to choose to share with them the issues that we need help with. You can only obtain true freedom when you choose it for yourself. Freedom will never be created when you have a person of authority breathing down your neck and trying to keep you clean. This will only lead to resentfulness and more hiddenness. We all need Fathers, Mothers and prophetic friends in our lives to help us reach a place of initially seeing where we have missed the mark, sinned, or stepped into wrong behaviors and shame.

However, that is not the place in which we are supposed to stay. David's sin with Bathsheba and his murder of her husband caused his heart to be hardened towards God for a short season. It took a prophet to confront him and point out his sin. But needing to have someone on the outside of our heart confront us with our issues is not the long-term plan of God to create healthy accountability in our lives. It is not a healthy relationship with God if I have to rely on others to constantly point out areas that I need growth in because I can't see them myself. We shouldn't have to get to the point where we don't hear God and have to get someone else to hear Him for us. That doesn't mean that I'm not thankful for those that have spoken into my blind spots and have helped bring me to the light when I was wandering a path of darkness; on the contrary, I am forever grateful for that. We all need people around us that will speak into those areas where we have allowed sin, shame or fear of being found out to cloud our relationship with God. I am simply saying that we also must be able to approach and hear God for ourselves too.

We have fought to create a culture that believes the best in people. In the overall picture, we are not looking for sin in people, but sin can never stay hidden. It seeks to destroy, shame, separate from relationship and create a mess and chaos wherever it goes. Sin is kept hidden for a season, but if a person doesn't choose to confess that issue before God and people, then it will be brought out into the light. It is actually for the good of that person's eternal place in God. Sin leads to death, but Jesus and walking in His ways brings life, eternal life. We want to get in the habit of being a people that chooses confession. I have chosen to develop that in my life over the course of 15 years and it has been what has kept me from jumping into stupid decisions and life-altering sins. I know that when I have demonic thoughts coming at me and I am beginning to believe those thoughts are mine I know I need help. I know I have to get those thoughts on the table in front of safe trusting people that I have built history with so that I can get free of them. Most of the time, they share with me that those thoughts do not line up with my identity or who I am. They give me wisdom to develop a better character in that given area and they also walk me through the process until I am free of that attack. They also dust the shame off of me and release His acceptance and forgiveness over me. Each time that I am faced with thoughts that could potentially turn into actions that are devastating, I choose to go to God, and then I must go to people to see full recovery. Repentance before God and man are the one two punch that takes out the enemy's ability to destroy God's people.

The Fruit of Repentance

The fourth part of this process is manifesting the fruit of repentance. Repentance is always demonstrated through changed behavior. Zacchaeus was a good example of this. He was a tax collector who dishonestly stole from many people. But when he had a revelation of unconditional love and acceptance by Jesus wanting to spend time with him, true repentance came.

Luke 19:8-10,

> "But Zacchaeus stood up and said to the Lord, 'Look, Lord! Here and now I give half of my possessions to the poor, and if I have cheated anybody out of anything, I will pay back four times the amount.' Jesus said to him, 'Today salvation has come to this house, because this man, too, is a son of Abraham. For the Son of Man came to seek and to save what was lost.'"

Many people confess their sins in private or at an altar, but do not enter into an improved lifestyle. A change in lifestyle can only be obtained through help from others. Sometimes people say, "Well, the grace of God does everything."

Yes, the grace of God does everything; but the grace of God requires people to bring it to pass and it requires action to manifest sustainable freedom. Paul makes it clear in 1 Corinthians 15:10,

> "But by the grace of God I am what I am, and his grace to me was not without effect. No, I worked harder than all of them - yet not I, but the grace of God that was with me."

In Titus 2, Paul tells Titus that he must teach people how to live rightly, and then he ends the chapter sharing that the grace of God teaches people. So, the grace of God is seen through the teaching, whether it is public preaching or one-on-one interaction and mentorship.

Titus 2:1, "You must teach what is in accord with sound doctrine. Teach the older men to be temperate, worthy of respect, self-controlled, and sound in faith, in love and in endurance...."

Titus 2:11, "For the grace of God that brings salvation has appeared to all men. It teaches us..."

Just as much as we must partner with God to see His grace resulting in a changed lifestyle, we also need teaching to impart the needed grace to change. Teaching through the help of people is actually a release of grace. Embracing people that help us develop a strategy for bearing the fruit of repentance means that it brings us to a different place in our character. Most often, changed character will only be sustainable in a culture of Fathers and Mothers. As they help train and release the grace of God through teaching, we are able to walk in a different lifestyle. John the Baptist showed the way of repentance and declared this powerful phrase in Luke 3:8, "Produce fruit in keeping with repentance."

I've witnessed my share of folks that carry the kind of attitude that says, well God's grace covers a multitude of sins, so I can do whatever I want. No, His grace does not cover sin. He requires us to not stay in our sins if we want to house His presence. When the people asked John what producing fruit was all about, He gave them some markers to demonstrate the tangible fruit of repentance. Luke 3:10-14 says,

> "'What should we do then?' the crowd asked.
> John answered, 'The man with two tunics should share with him who has none, and the one who has food should do the same.'
> Tax collectors also came to be baptized. 'Teacher,' they asked, 'what should we do?'
> 'Don't collect any more than you are required to,' he told them.
> Then some soldiers asked him, 'And what should we do?'
> He replied, 'Don't extort money and don't accuse people falsely — be content with your pay.'"

Empowered to Live Differently

Now you might think that was before Jesus and they were still under the law. I would say the laws and behaviors of heaven have never changed. Jesus didn't take away from us the need to walk in moral behavior. He gave the power to live out moral behavior and right attitudes from within our hearts. The law moved from the outside to the inside, but we actually never got rid of the law. The law has always been love. Everything that we are to do and not to do is captured in love. Love is found in Jesus, and Jesus is now in us. We have the power to walk in love. Jesus in us does not give us the freedom to sin. I don't know why people would want to see how close to the sin fence they can get and still be saved. I don't want to have anything to do with the devastating effects of sin. I know that it's His power in me that keeps me free, but I also know that part of that power in me is created through people around me that I must confess to. I need Fathers and Mothers helping me to develop processes that help me walk out the fruit of repentance on a daily basis until I can sustain that new freedom. Freedom is sustainable through repetition. Repetition is created through consistent relational encounters with loving people who carry the Father's heart for me.

Continually remembering what Jesus did for us and to us is a part of creating sustainable freedom in us. Maintaining an intimate relationship with Jesus our King while being overwhelmed by His goodness and presence is another key to staying soft and sensitive to His voice. In that place of intimacy, we must protect His wonderful presence and anything that gets in the way of the sweetness of His constant presence must be eliminated from our lives.

Walking Us Into Healing

Having people that can walk us into healing through confession is key for our establishment of true freedom. Embracing and welcoming Fathers and Mothers in our midst who can teach us how to create strongholds of godly character in our lives is key to our long-term success. These are all a part of the process of repentance that sets us up for long-term victory. God wants to create cultures in our midst where there are not just a few that carry the Father's heart but many who can be a part of leading people to confession and establishment of freedom. He wants an army! An army of motherly and fatherly people who create a culture that produces a harvest of prodigal sons and daughters longing to be free, accepted and healed. We have not been able to sustain a harvest because we don't have Fathering cultures created in our churches. You can only be trusted with the amount of people you are prepared to handle. You can have large churches where many people are saved, but living in torment of hidden bondages and shame. We want to see multitudes that are saved, healed, delivered, free and walking in wonderful family relationships of true freedom.

In order to begin to create a Kingdom culture of true freedom, we must embrace a culture of repentance. We need to be courageous enough to find fathers, mothers and trustworthy friends that model the heart of Dad's loving acceptance. We also need to be fearless enough to embrace our role to release the Father's heart to others as well. As we learn to persevere with people and help them to bring forth the fruit of repentance, we will need to clearly see the Father for who He really is. In the next chapter, I want to bring us into an awareness of who this present reformation's view of God is. As we see Him so we will be like Him. When we are manifesting His likeness, there will be no one that compares to us, for we are His church, the bride.

Chapter 5

Embracing The Present Reformation's View Of God

Any sustainable transformation or reformation must first begin with a fresh revelation of God. Every move of God that we have seen has created patterns that shifted how church was done and how people did life. The church buildings created during those eras are a reflection of that season's view of God. For example, the pulpits shifting to center stage came from a view that God's word was to be communicated in the language of all people, not just a select educated few. Platforms for playing music came from the freedom that was fought for to express the songs of the movements of the reformation of the past. These and other external changes came out of fresh perspectives of God in times of needed upgrade in the church.

Dimensions of God

Often the structure and arrangements within our church buildings are actually a direct reflection of our internal view of God. Modernized buildings that removed traditional pews and put chairs in their place came from a fresh view of God. That change was an expression of the people feeling like they could begin to relax around God. Being in His house wasn't as scary as previously projected. There could be more access for everyone and He could be easily reached. You could be in His presence and actually be comfortable.

In addition to building structure changes, each change in song style is also a reflection of the fresh view of God people encountered. As hymns brought people into an awareness of His majesty, choruses allowed people to enter into a greater awareness of His nearness. Every move of God begins to unveil another dimension of God's character, and we see that displayed externally in our physical environments.

So what does the building look like where you gather to worship? What do the physical features say about your view of God? Is the style consistent with that view? Does the place need a face-lift?

If you believe God is distant, then in seating you will create distance between yourself and others. How you view God will manifest in how you engage people in meetings or in one-on-one conversation. If you believe God is tender towards you, then you will tend to create more intimate settings for people to engage God. I know that anything I see in God, I will manifest in the world around me. That is why I am so enthralled in knowing Him. I know that any sustainable breakthrough comes first from an increased awareness of another side of Him I haven't seen before. Knowing Him fully is the goal. The right revelation of God and who He is will affect every part of my life just as much as a distorted view of God will negatively impact my life. As I encounter Him, then the physical surroundings I meet within need to line up with what I believe about Him.

The Father and the Bridegroom

I remember hearing someone say that God is so incredibly patient. He said it takes God around four hundred years to get mad. God is so incredibly patient! I immediately thought, well that same God is in me and if He is in me, then I need to be more patient with my family and people around me. I grew up reciting the fruits of the spirit from memory. But that day, I actually received the revelation of God's patience that totally rocked me. Especially since I know that anything I see in Him, I am invited into the character and reality of that truth. 1 John 4:17 says it like this, "Because in this world we are like him."

Through this passage, God is inviting me into a greater discovery of who He is. One aspect of Him that I love to meditate upon is God as King. In my awareness of Him as my King, I walk in a greater place of authority to manifest His Kingdom here on earth. He is King with authority over His kingdom. Therefore, I am a King with authority to bring His kingdom to earth. His nature declares my identity. That is why it is important to recognize and to define what nature He is demonstrating to us. This is what He wants to manifest in us. In light of that revelation, we must then create a culture around us that aligns with that revelation. Revelation must become reality or it is simply information that inflates us without changing us.

Over the last twenty years as a corporate body, who has God been revealing Himself to us as? Two of the main identities I've seen Him reveal of Himself is Father and Bridegroom. In this last season, it's very possible that He has revealed something else to you, which is wonderful. I love to discover, explore and hear about every view of God that His people see about Him. I want every part of Him and I believe that our distinct views of His reality in our lives is the inheritance in the saints we all get to share in. Every person has a view of God from his or her personal history in God and each of us has a slightly different angle in Him. Obviously, all of this should absolutely line up with biblical foundations so as to not wander down a wrong path.

Revealing the Father

The view that He is a Father, a daddy, has been a primary revelation in the last 20 years of church. This is how He revealed Himself when Jesus came to earth over 2,000 years ago. Jesus spoke repeatedly declaring that He was here to reveal and speak on behalf of the Father. In John 14, and in many other places, Jesus speaks that His main purpose was to reveal the Father. John 14:9-14,

> "Jesus answered: 'Don't you know me, Philip, even after I have been among you such a long time? Anyone who has seen me has seen the Father. How can you say, *'Show us the Father?'* Don't you believe that I am in the Father, and that the Father is in me? The words I say to you are not just my own. Rather, it is the Father, living in me, who is doing his work. Believe me when I say that I am in the Father and the Father is in me; or at least believe on the evidence of the miracles themselves. I tell you the truth, anyone who has faith in me will do what I have been doing. He will do even greater things than these, because I am going to the Father. And I will do whatever you ask in my name, so that the Son may bring glory to the Father.'"

It was the Father who sent the Son to the world. He sent His Son to the world and He is looking for sons and daughters to manifest His character. Father God is looking for a family and He has been saturating us with His heart as a Father so we could then learn to generate what He has created in our hearts. He desires for His lost loved ones to be able to come into the home atmosphere we create. Heaven's atmosphere on earth is a place of safety, acceptance, vulnerability, trust, love, redemption and truth; where nothing needs to be hidden. It is a place where a Father is present.

We need Fathers and Mothers that are drenched in the revelation that Daddy God is a wonderful, safe and approachable Father. These Fathers and Mothers need to have experienced Father God through heavenly encounters. They also need to have experienced Father God's character through their own spiritual Fathers. We need every person to carry the revelation of a good Dad within their spirits so that whether they are a son, friend, father, mother, brother, or even sister in how they relate to one another, they can model the Father. This will then create a contagious culture that the prodigals will run home to. This is the atmosphere that must be within us as we are accessing the seven mountains and moving into power and prophetic evangelism.

Love Evangelism

We need to demonstrate love evangelism. Love evangelism is letting your light shine before men with such love, truth, acceptance and vulnerability that pre-Christians can't help but say they want the heavenly dad they see in us welcomed into their lives. The level at which we see and know God is the level at which we witness to people from. Our revelation becomes an authentic expression through our lives and can either attract or repel people into or out of an experience with God.

The outflow of a revelation of Him as Dad must cause us to change the way we conduct our corporate gatherings, whether in homes or buildings. We need to manifest what a truly heavenly culture of family would look like. He died for His sons and daughters, which opened up our heavenly home for us to access now. Heaven isn't a cold stone castle built of fine materials. Heaven is a warm embrace while seeing the Father's tender smile. This is illustrated in the book of John, chapter 14:1-4,

"Do not let your hearts be troubled. Trust in God; trust also in me. In my Father's house are many rooms; if it were not so, I would have told you. I am going there to prepare a place for you. And if I go and prepare a place for you, I will come back and take you to be with me that you also may be where I am. You know the way to the place where I am going."

Jesus isn't speaking about preparing a place for us when we die. He is actually speaking about a place we can access now. The good news here is that we don't have to wait! Ephesians 2:6 says that we have been seated with Christ in this place, "And God raised us up with Christ and seated us with him in the heavenly realms in Christ Jesus." We have been given access to the house of God, which is a home. However, most of our services and buildings emulate an Old Testament model of God. Our meetings reflect something that is not congruent to the nature of God that we have been declaring. Often times, we are declaring a view of heavenly Father in a very non-fatherly way and atmosphere. It's a dichotomy, like speaking about the gentleness of God with a harsh edge. The contradiction is keeping the transfer of truth from penetrating into the hearts of the people.

Who are You?

I have heard it said in many ways, that you speak what you know but you impart who you are. So who are you? You are a direct reflection of your view of who God is. Are you satisfied in the way you are modeling God through your character, life-example, and words? Are you satisfied with the way God is modeled in your church services? Are you satisfied in the God you are consistently demonstrating and talking about in your spheres of influence? Is your environment congruent with whom you are declaring Him to be in you? I know that God has many facets of His nature. He is the lion and the lamb. He is the prince of peace and the God who has the sword coming out of His mouth to conquer His enemies. He is love and He is judge. All of these truths are harmonious and perfectly coincide, even though the truths seem opposing. So what is the overarching view of God being revealed to you?

God has so many aspects to explore. Just one facet of Him will take us such a great distance in our journey of knowing Him. Another component of Him will invite us into another great adventure altogether. He is the eternal epic adventure. We need to continually press into Him as our Father, and discover how approachable He really is.

Enter the Bridegroom

We also get to embrace Him as the Bridegroom. This is another major manifestation of God that He is restoring to the church. Sometimes one view of God can take us into one dimension of Him and if we are to explore more aspects of His character, we need a different unfolding of who He is. My picture of God as Dad revealed many treasures to me. Yet it was another side of God altogether that revealed His tenderness. As I saw Him as the Bridegroom, I experienced tenderness like never before. This tenderness showed me a softer and sweeter side of God. As I experienced tenderness from Him as bridegroom, my personality also changed. As we are changed then we are able to bring others into that change.

Creating An Environment

In our youth meetings over the last few months, we experimented with setting up physical environments that relay these two facets of God; Father and bridegroom. We created a space that appeared and felt like a family living room, but also set up a dining room with a banqueting table. Both of these dynamics created unique expressions and experiences that invited us into encounters of these two different views of God.

I love the picture of Jesus as lovingly generous. To express this, we set up a series of tables filled with fruits, nuts and goodies. We then decorated them with candles. To wrap it up with finishing touches, we surrounded the area with curtains. We then played intimate worship music during the gathering time and took communion together. The youth were invited to eat whatever they desired from the tables. We had prepared the tables with so much food that there was more than enough for everyone. Each of the youth experienced such a genuine excitement over the food that was lavished upon them. This was really just a small display of the One who is captivated with love for us.

Fresh Biblical Perspective

As we continue to find more ways to be congruent with the message of who He is, we will also have to find ways to see scripture with fresh perspective. I love reading Song of Solomon through the Message Bible. The language of that translation is personal and warm. The language of other Bible translations that we read often does not exude the heart of who God is. Often times they feel so business-like, which can create distance and confusion. It is difficult to understand God's endearing heart in some of the old English works. I am provoked to see the Bible written more and more in the language of the Father and the Son and how they would be expressing it to us as a Dad and a loving husband in modern day terminology and language. We must know Him as both Dad and husband to fully grasp His love for us. In addition, our character must become congruent with that of our Father and Husband so that we can exude this nature of Him to others.

Family Business

Sometimes, I travel to nations where I am asked to do ministry. The ministry feels more like a transaction rather than a family interaction. I am expected to preach and prophesy a certain number of times. Each time I preach, a pre-determined, set amount is given to me. The amounts that I get paid to preach are a fixed fee just like a job would be. I appreciate the precision and clarity of this type of agreement and understand that there is the practical side of ministry at times. However, I also wonder if there is a way that our interactions couldn't be more like a family doing business with each other. We are not running impersonal business in which we are expected to produce a product, rather we are helping serve His house of which there is business involved. That means our hearts must be connected in everything we do. How would we do business with someone who we are family with? When you see someone as family, the way you handle the business side of things becomes more personal rather than transactional. Our relational values must manifest in everything we do.

Heavenly Family Dynamics

Looking at another angle, why are interactions with people from our congregations often times more transactional than relational? If we were authentically a family, would we fire our misbehaving employees or treat them as sons needing adjustments? If necessary, would you then send him off in tears because of his inability to honor the way of life at his job? Would you write him off when he had outlived his function or would he forever be in your heart? If we truly see people as family, then we are not going to be able to get rid of them the way we have in the past. There may be a time and place to let people go from a job, but it is how we do it that matters most.

Often times we treat blood family different then we treat the family of God around us. There isn't the same level of covenant with the body of Christ as there is with our own family. The one thing I know about blood family is that they are always with you, in good and bad circumstances. The perplexing thing I discovered about the church is often times, function is more important than relationship. For example, with blood family relatives, when it comes time for the holidays, it doesn't matter how much we agree on the doctrines and beliefs of the church; we still get together and enjoy some good food and laughs together. When will the body of Christ, the family of God, begin to protect our relationships in the same manner? When the end of the day comes are we still going to be enjoying each other relationally and not just functionally? Are we connected only to hear sermons and receive and give tithes or are we connected for life?

I do realize the difficulty in including everyone in our personal lives, but eternally we are one large family. There are many families that connect and overlap with other families, building one entirely large Christian family. We all have one and the same daddy. Ephesians 3:14-15 says it this way, "For this reason I kneel before the Father, from whom his whole family in heaven and on earth derives its name." Ephesians 2:19 also says, "Consequently, you are no longer foreigners and aliens, but fellow citizens with God's people and members of God's household..."

We must transition from people who only declare with our words that we are family to manifesting the characteristics of true heavenly family. It is time to manifest the behaviors of family with each other. In addition, we must change from being people who only declare with our words that we are the bride into having experienced Him as a bride. We must be people that have encountered His tender, loving eyes and gentle lips speaking to us. From that place of revelation we must manifest the tender, loving, caring and gentle culture through us to everyone around us.

I love how the message Bible reveals Jesus the bridegroom and speaks of Him in Song of Solomon 5:12, "His eyes are like doves, soft and bright, but deep-set, brimming with meaning, like wells of water." and 5:16, "His words are kisses, his kisses words. Everything about him delights me, thrills me through and through!"

Taking It Personal

Every time I see a new side of Him in scripture, in my spirit, or even through the words and life of another, I am provoked to internalize that reality of Him. I understand that I am a new creation in which He lives. I know that as I see more clearly the One that fully resides in me, then I will more fully manifest Him in my life. The goal is to continue to receive the revelation of who God is through the five-fold ministry and the saints until we are fully manifesting His beautiful nature on earth. Then we will be a bride that is in equal proportion to Him in every way. The glory and power that we are designed to carry is beyond words.

Ephesians 4:11-15,

"It was he who gave some to be apostles, some to be prophets, some to be evangelists, and some to be pastors and teachers, to prepare God's people for works of service, so that the body of Christ may be built up until we all reach unity in the faith and in the knowledge of the Son of God and become mature, attaining to the whole measure of the fullness of Christ. Then we will no longer be infants, tossed back and forth by the waves, and blown here and there by every wind of teaching and by the cunning and craftiness of men in their deceitful scheming. Instead, speaking the truth in love, we will in all things grow up into him who is the Head, that is, Christ."

It's very exciting that God is committed to growing us into the fullness of His Son. What a wonderful joy it will be when the sons of God are manifesting the nature of the Father and the Bridegroom on earth. In the next chapter I want to explore the characteristics of a true son. Those who know the Son of God who lives within them will walk as sons of God on earth.

Chapter 6

Transforming Into
Fully Manifested Sons Of God

Our Daddy is a Spirit and He is looking for spiritual sons on earth to reveal Himself through. Those who intimately know who their heavenly Daddy is will be mighty and will accomplish many great and heroic deeds on the earth. Daniel 11:32 in the KJV says it this way, "but the people that do know their God shall be strong, and do exploits." God's desire is to have relationship with sons and daughters who bring in His reign upon the earth. He has given us everything we need. He wants us to enjoy living in the revelation that He takes care of His own. There is no need to struggle to access heaven's blessings. We have no need to run outside of relationship with Him to find anything. Everything is found in Him. He is our eternal source.

Prodigals

In the story of the prodigal son, the two sons are both bankrupt in heart. One took his inheritance and left his Father. He tried to use the gifts he received to make himself a name and eventually he became impoverished. The other lived and worked at the family farm, but never accessed all that was his. He thought his work ethic and dedication was what qualified him to be a son. He never realized that he too was an orphan. He needed the Father to remind him of what belonged to him and whose he was. In Luke 15:31 we hear the Father declare, "My son you are always with me, and everything I have is yours."

When we are learning to become sons, we may currently manifest one of the two ways that these sons operated in around their Father. They were both functioning outside of relationship and were trying to earn favor and access through what they did and what they had. It wasn't about their relationship with their Father, but rather based on performance. God often teaches us how to stay in relationship with Him by connecting us to a local family, a part of the body of Christ. This local church body is our family, and it is to our benefit to view and treat it that way. We all know that churches can have problems, just like any organization of people can. However imperfect the local body is, and no matter what changes we feel need to be implemented for improvement, God has allowed it to be what it is. This helps us to develop a sense of sonship and belonging to a family. The best of families are imperfect but are still God's place for sons to learn covenant relationship. Do you have a local group of healthy believers and a leadership that you connect with and submit to on a regular basis?

No Longer Orphans

In America, I have noticed and personally struggled with a mindset of individuality. It is the mindset that says "If I don't get anything out of this for me, then I'm not doing it" or "I have to get a breakthrough for myself, because no one else is going to do it for me." This is actually a poverty mindset and an orphan spirit in action that must be broken in the body if we are to truly allow the reformation to flow through our lives. We must ask ourselves, are we really in a Kingdom family or not? Many would say, well I trust God, but I don't trust the dads and moms that are in the faith around me. Or some would say I trust some of the people some of the time, but never all the time. Ultimately, our heavenly Dad is our Dad where we get our affirmation, encouragement, comfort, identity and direction. But we will not be able to get to our destination unless we become true sons of God. True sons of God are formed in the body of Christ. Galatians 4:6-7 says,

> "Because you are sons, God sent the Spirit of his Son into our hearts, the Spirit who calls out, 'Abba, Father.' So you are no longer a slave, but a son; and since you are a son, God has made you also an heir."

Since we are no longer orphans, we are meant to maintain a family mindset. An orphan spirit tries to get what it can from the family and then stops protecting the relationship when something better comes along. A healthy and balanced family mindset believes that you are in the body for life, and that together you are of mutual benefit, even when it may not feel good. An orphan spirit manifests in people who roam from place to place using their gifts to gain acceptance until it's time to move on again. This could be due to rejection, boredom, or many other reasons. However, a family mindset is committed to a local body of believers until Jesus sends him or her somewhere else for another strategic purpose.

What Motivates Us?

Our motivation in finding a new place should be based on Father God telling us where we should go. We are to be located where we find a body of believers that feels like home. Moving churches should not be directed by external circumstances, such as finding a different job, unless of course, God is orchestrating your move in that way. We stay or move based on our identity and purpose within family. There are many places and churches that I personally enjoy visiting, and they even feel like close relatives. But not every place that I go is my home. I can create a home environment and be a part of a family everywhere I go, since we are a part of one big kingdom family. Ultimately, however, I am called to walk out my daily life at one place that I call home. The place where I reside is where I have earthly fathers and mothers that model the Heavenly Father to me. Additionally, I should find earthly brothers and sisters in the spirit that I work in partnership with to expand our Father's kingdom.

During a recent ministry trip in which I experienced a heightened level of warfare, I noticed the individual mindset in my own life and the damage it can cause. I had been invited to speak at a church in the Washington, D.C. area, and my family was able to come with me. We were all very excited about it, since this is our nation's capitol. Despite our excitement, this trip seemed to be nothing but hardship and trouble from the very beginning. Our initial flights were canceled and we had to pay for hotel rooms until we could secure a flight out the next day to D.C. We didn't have the money at the time, so this was quite a burden for us. The next day, we arrived in D.C. and the atmosphere was tense. We experienced problem after problem while we were there, although we chose to make the most out of it. Even on our drive home from the airport, our luggage flew off of the car and we had to recover it off the freeway.

I couldn't figure out what was going on. This is not the way things are supposed to be. I know at times we hit spiritual turbulence, but man this was too much. It wasn't until the last day of the trip when we were flying into the San Francisco airport when God told me why it had been such a difficult trip. He told me that I went there on my own. He said you didn't go as one being sent from your local body, but you went in your own authority. I thought to myself, "How can this be? The local team of leaders had previously blessed me and laid hands on me to travel as an itinerant minister." I always did the best I could to make sure the leaders over me were aware of what I was doing. I stayed in connection with them concerning my schedule. But the Lord said, "You must pull them into your heart and come into the revelation that you are not building your own ministry. You are building mine as well as adding to the ministry of your home church."

I didn't realize that I had entered a mindset that declared that I was going on my own. I thought that if I don't make something happen for my family and me, nothing would happen. I couldn't see that I was just trying to use my local church to help get me ahead and didn't have their hearts close to mine. From that point on, I tried to pull them into my heart as I traveled and I made sure to have them lay hands on me before I went anywhere. Most importantly of all, I tried to keep the mindset that I am here to help my local family succeed; instead of thinking I am here to make things happen only for myself.

Sometimes I have thought that if I don't create a ministry for myself, it won't happen. I know I am responsible to build what He has given me but I am to be building with a team mindset as my focus. I have also thought that I may not be here at this local church forever and if I leave, I better make sure I have a sustainable ministry outside of the church. These are good plans, but the motivation behind them can be impure. For me personally, this was a mindset that needed to shift since it's one that wasn't based in trust.

It is amazing that you can get through an inheritance what it may have taken years and years to get on your own. If I shift my mindset and believe that I am simply here to serve whom the Father has put in my path, then I trust that God will promote me in the way I need to be promoted and at the right time. At different times over the last years, I have chosen to serve in areas where my primary focus wasn't high. However, choosing to serve there became the very door that opened me up to greater levels of favor and promotion into the dreams of my heart.

Power of Team

It has been difficult for me to break through the mentality that I have to build something on my own. Orphans build alone, but sons build in team. I have spent the last six years at The Mission in Vacaville learning the absolute necessity of team. The value of working in a team capacity is invaluable. There have been tears and hardships, but I would not want it any other way. It is so wonderful to not be primarily in charge of every ministry and to be required to function in all of the areas of service. Rather, I can function within the areas that I have gifting in and the ministries that I have been given to develop, and then let others develop the areas that apply to them respectively.

In this atmosphere of team, I then get to enjoy the wonderful privilege of discovering the heartbeat of the local fathers that I serve. It is my joy to find out what it is they burn for and to discover a way to help them advance that. I am a dreamer and at times I dream of running large ministries of significant influence with thousands of people. It is then the Lord reminds me that if I help the fathers in my life succeed in their dreams, then out of that success, what I am dreaming has greater potential to be realized.

Timing is the essence of our dreams. It is funny that the things I am helping build now are actually what I dreamed of building fifteen years ago. I received certain prophetic words fifteen years ago and was frustrated that they did not come to pass when they were given. It seems when finally I let go of my striving and performance, those things fell into my lap. Fifteen years later here I am walking in some of those words. Had I received the fullness of those words then, I wouldn't have been ready. Now I am much more confident in the areas that I have been given. I'm no longer mesmerized with the words spoken. I am walking them out faithfully, bearing fruit for the Kingdom, and serving those that He has put before me to serve.

We Are A Family

In your physical family, there are times that you do things because they need to get done. This contributes to the functionality of the family structure and everybody has chores to complete to keep the house clean and tidy. Since we are also a church family, we could even say that we serve the house and the Fathers that He has put in our lives to serve. We serve as a method to help His vision succeed. It's amazing that when a son truly serves a Father with pure motives and without a hidden agenda looking for promotion, he actually gets promoted in ways he could never have on his own.

The reformation upon us is producing a family mindset that breaks us out of independent mindsets that cripple. There are times we get to chase our personal dreams, but I like to see my personal dreams as one part of a greater corporate dream puzzle. Ultimately, my dream is one piece of our heavenly Daddy's big dream. Sonship is what we are after, not fame. We need fathers that breed identity and not performance to cause us to walk securely in our part of the larger picture.

When we are living with a true sonship mindset, we are not trying to get someone's position. We are also not waiting for the Father to die or retire so we can get our inheritance and take his position. Neither are we fighting with our brothers for our shot at the limelight. There are plenty of significant opportunities for all of us at the table of the Lord. There is more than enough inheritance and rich rewards. I don't want my Father's spot. I want my own spot. Of course I want to receive the wisdom and experience that the Fathers have. I want to walk with them, helping carry out their dreams and visions. I also want the dreams of my heart to come to pass. When I learn to truly honor and serve the Fathers that the Lord gives me, then I will receive a double portion. That double portion will be walking in all the wonderful benefits that I have gleaned from them as well as what the Lord has given me personally. Then I can expand and take what is being built beyond what my Father's legacy looked like.

Building Generationally

Truly, it is a Father's greatest joy to see his sons outdo him. Personally, I am extremely delighted that my children are experiencing aspects of the Spirit of God that I didn't even know existed until I was in my twenties. They have accessed the prophetic, healing, hearing God and even worship; all at a higher level then I did in my childhood. I thank the Lord for that and I am looking to help them to continue to grow spiritually.

In addition to what they are now walking in, I want to see their dreams come true. If they are to see their dreams fulfilled, first I have to know that they are trustworthy. A father wants to give to his children what they desire and he will help them succeed when he sees that they are trustworthy. He is waiting to see that the sons and daughters protect his heart and honor what is important to him as their father. When children receive what the fathers have been revealing to them, then the father will go to great lengths to serve what the child needs. He will want him or her to take their dreams beyond the experience of his personal dreams.

The most important process that we must go through in becoming sons is to become trustworthy. First we become trustworthy by trusting those that God has given us. You can never be a son that builds something with a Father if you don't trust him. Trusting someone means we allow him or her to take us places we have no understanding of. We allow them to speak into us and provide us with insights that we don't or can't see. We don't question and resist them every step of the way, but we welcome their feedback. Proverbs says this of our walk with God in chapter 3 verses 5-6,

> "Trust in the Lord with all your heart
> and lean not on your own understanding;
> in all your ways acknowledge him,
> and he will make your paths straight."

Preparing Us For Our Heart's Desires

We are all called to fall back into the arms of a good dad and allow him to lead us into things that we may feel uncertain of what's next. Sometimes we are serving in areas that seem so far from what we desire, but we fail to realize they are actually training us for the dreams of our heart. Joseph probably didn't realize his training with Potiphar and his wife, the jail and it's prisoners, and the lessons he learned as a son with his father and brothers were all preparing him for his dream to be fulfilled. Each of these seasons prepared him to handle the inheritance handed over to him by Pharaoh. He learned to honor the dream of Pharaoh, and because of that, he brought reality to the dream of his family and God's plan for the Israelites to eventually come into their promised land. Egypt was a safe haven that preserved the promised people until they had outgrown the capacity available in the Promised Land. I am certain that Joseph had little idea that his life would result in such an important step towards the dream of his forefathers coming true.

Don't Miss Blessings in Disguise

I have observed that sometimes we live with such shortsightedness that we can easily and quickly shut down a blessing in disguise. We often try to escape difficulties in circumstances and relationships instead of facing the personal issues that arise that need to be dealt with. We sometimes try to separate ourselves from people that think or behave out of a different set of core values than our own. We may not realize that as we begin to see these people from heaven's perspective, the very things we were trying to escape were actually important steps in the preparation for our success. If we had welcomed them instead of fought them the whole way, who knows what increased blessings we would have realized.

The First Commandment That Comes With A Blessing

It is wonderful when the sons honor the fathers in a way that accelerates the fathers' dreams. Whether the fathers are restoring their hearts to the sons or the sons are restoring their hearts to the fathers, one truth is certain. We can break the curse off of our inheritance by honoring both fathers and sons. This in turn can cause resistant sons and/or fathers to restore their honor to us. Malachi 4:5-6 says,

> "See, I will send you the prophet Elijah before that great and dreadful day of the Lord comes. He will turn the hearts of the fathers to their children, and the hearts of the children to their fathers; or else I will come and strike the land with a curse."

Blessings Not Curses

I believe that God wants to break a financial curse off of the land. It is a physical curse on our belongings, our livelihood, our jobs, homes, physical bodies, cities and even our nations. As we begin to learn how to be sons, we will draw out the Father in others. In learning to be sons, we will learn how to be fathers. Sons are needed to restore the earth, not just good ministers. Romans 8:19-21 says,

"The creation waits in eager expectation for the sons of God to be revealed. For the creation was subjected to frustration, not by its own choice, but by the will of the one who subjected it, in hope that the creation itself will be liberated from its bondage to decay and brought into the glorious freedom of the children of God."

We have to transform how we see ourselves and those that carry the Father's heart around us if we are to see creation restored to freedom. Our original purpose on earth has always been to rule and subdue the earth within an intimate relationship with God. Genesis 1:28 says,

"God blessed them and said to them, 'Be fruitful and increase in number; fill the earth and subdue it. Rule over the fish of the sea and the birds of the air and over every living creature that moves on the ground.'"

Sonship Restoration In Five Fold Ministry

As we grow in awareness of the reformation that is upon us, we will realize that everything God gave us was in order to restore us to true sonship. The main purpose of the gifts of the Spirit wasn't to wow us or make us feel significant or powerful as a minister, but to be an extension of our heavenly Father's desire to bring His sons and daughters back to Him. Reaching people isn't about souls as much as it's about fathers pursuing lost sons and daughters. Our heavenly Dad wants us to carry His heartbeat and to use what gifts He has given us to communicate from that place. He is looking to restore His family. Luke 15:4-7 reflects this truth,

> "Suppose one of you has a hundred sheep and loses one of them. Does he not leave the ninety-nine in the open country and go after the lost sheep until he finds it? And when he finds it, he joyfully puts it on his shoulders and goes home. Then he calls his friends and neighbors together and says, 'Rejoice with me; I have found my lost sheep. 'I tell you that in the same way there will be more rejoicing in heaven over one sinner who repents than over ninety-nine righteous persons who do not need to repent."

When we explore the five-fold gifts of Apostle, Prophet, Teacher, Pastor and Evangelist, we can see that the Father's heart is communicated through each of them. The gifts essentially help establish healthy sons and daughters in the faith. In this present reformation, Apostles should carry His heart to establish cultures of heavenly family and model a father. Prophets carry the spirit of Elijah and have a heart to declare the messages needed to restore the fathers and mothers to their children. They remove stumbling blocks that hinder relationships with our Heavenly Father and earthly family. They model the atmosphere of heaven's family here on earth. This then creates a culture of safety where the children can gain identity, security and purpose.

Five-fold teachers should operate as Paul the teacher and apostle who declared in 1 Corinthians 4:15, "For though ye have ten thousand instructors in Christ, yet have ye not many fathers: for in Christ Jesus I have begotten you through the gospel."

The goal of teachers should be to model the Heavenly Father and to speak as a father would, which includes imparting revelation into sons and daughters that breathes into them who God's word says they are.

The aim of true five-fold pastors is to bring the lost sons and daughters back into the flock while also creating cultures that heal relationships and draws people out of orphan hearts and into fullness of health. We need pastors that draw back in the sheep that have fallen away. We also need pastors that can create cultures where everyone begins to think in terms of family, restoration, reconciliation, protecting love, fighting for one another, believing the best in each other, looking for gold, etc.

Finally, the purpose of the five-fold evangelist is to carry Dad's heart for those who are outside the fold as well as imparting to the body of believers a heart for every tribe, tongue and person on the planet. We can't have the mindset that writes people off. Evangelists should implore us all to carry Dad's heart for every prodigal person and to see him or her as a dad would see his child.

Carrying the Father's Heart

I went through a season in which everywhere I went was training my heart to realize that every person I saw or encountered was actually someone's son or daughter. Sometimes we watch movies or see the news and our hearts want justice for the good guy and want the bad guys punished or dead. We want those who are fighting against our rights to be dealt with and want punishment for those that have broken the laws. But if you put yourself in a different perspective and simply think, "If this was my child, what would I want for them? Would I want that criminal or terrorist from another country or my own country to be killed or punished?" Ultimately, we don't want to generalize people out of prejudice or fear. Would we want to see someone punished if we saw him or her as God's son or daughter? I'm not saying that prison or earthly justice isn't necessary for those that break laws. I am asking us to consider what drives us to want justice and what causes us to dehumanize an individual who is acting poorly.

God is going to entrust a large harvest to those who carry His heart. I remember a time I was in Korea and I was praying that God would touch these people with His love. I felt nothing in my prayer or heart. When I changed my prayer and began to pray with a different language and focus to "Oh God, touch my people, my Koreans," then I suddenly felt His pleasure. He wanted me to bring them into my heart and see them as an extension of my family. He won't give us anybody that we can't get our hearts around. But He will entrust us with those that we get our hearts around.

What Matters To The Father

As sons and daughters, we are responsible to care for what the Father cares for, feel for what the Father feels for, protect what the Father protects, build what the Father is building, and love what the Father loves. God's kingdom isn't a stone castle with a distant King. God's kingdom has an ever-present Dad who is living in the home of our hearts as believers. He wants to make Himself known through us to everyone on this planet. He is constantly in pursuit of His lost family. We are the sons and daughters who are here on earth to display His heart to all those we come into contact with. If our prayer is "on earth as it is in heaven," then we have to begin to create family in the environments that we serve. Ultimately, we are serving the heavenly Father's vision and that vision is that the whole world would know His love. John 3:16-17 says it so clearly,

"For God so loved the world that he gave his one and only Son, that whoever believes in him shall not perish but have eternal life. For God did not send his Son into the world to condemn the world, but to save the world through him."

It was a good Father's desire to see the human race restored with their Heavenly Father, and so He sent His son. He didn't send His Son to judge and so it's not our job to judge or condemn. It's our job as sons who have Jesus Christ the Son of God inside of us to model the Father's heart wherever we go. It's also our job to fulfill His dream, expand His kingdom, and invite many into His eternal home. As we seek to expand His kingdom, He will certainly add everything to us with joy. Matthew 6:33, "But seek first his kingdom and his righteousness, and all these things will be given to you as well."

Impartation of Sonship

I declare over each of you that the spirit of sonship would rest on you. That you would feel the love of the Father, that you would be drawn into the warm embrace of heaven's acceptance over you. I further pray that you would enter into the revelation of Christ in you and would find your place as a son in the Kingdom and amongst a body of believers. Let each of you demonstrate the Father's heart and His values in every situation and setting that you walk into. I pray that you would exude acceptance, love, vulnerability, truth, wisdom, grace, gentleness, patience and kindness to all that you encounter, from the inside out. I pray that you step into the position of sonship that becomes so attractive to those on the outside of the family. I pray that lost people would knock on the doors of your houses, homes, jobs, church buildings and personal lives saying, "I want the light that I see in you." I declare that you are not an orphan, you are not fighting on your own, you are a part of a heavenly family, and you are fully accepted and loved. You are meant to be in the body and have a significant purpose in the family of God. You are your heavenly Father's child and He is your loving Dad.

In this chapter, I outlined a few of the markers that define spirit sons. In the next chapter, I will help define some of the markers to determine whether or not we are truly in family or not. Since family is what the church is reforming into, what are some of the markers that indicate we are on the right track in creating that culture?

Chapter 7

Signs Of A True Family

I f God is truly reforming the church from a house to a home, then we will need to explore the indicators of a healthy home. Most of us have experienced our share of dysfunction in our homes. To the contrary, some people have experienced healthy, happy environments at home. I want to define what a healthy spiritual family is by first looking at healthy biological families and home environments. Then we will examine how healthy we are as a spiritual family.

The reason we are looking for indicators to help define family is that these help us determine how we are doing in allowing our hearts to reform us towards what is on God's heart. Here are some questions for you to ponder as you read through this chapter: Do you have a healthy spiritual Father or Mother walking with you in this season? Are they available to you personally? Do you receive input from them? Do you allow yourself to become vulnerable around them? Have you stayed with them long enough to receive the inheritance they have to give to you? Allowing yourself to truthfully answer these questions will help you understand where you are at in your personal connection to Kingdom family.

Healthy Families

Let us explore together some obvious factors of healthy and whole families. This is not a complete list, as I am not attempting to create anything all-inclusive, but rather a good starting point. It is important for us each to determine the values in which we tether and base our relationships and decisions around as a group of believers.

One obvious sign of a healthy family is that there must be a father and a mother. Obviously God can do wonders with a single parent raising children. I am not overlooking His redemption. Rather, I am looking at His original design, which was a husband and wife raising children. In my earthly family, I have a wonderful mom and dad. No one can replace them. I have journeyed with them nearly 40 years. Some of those years I was living in their house, the first 18 years or so. The next 20 plus years, my parents and I connected from a variety of distances, sometimes living several thousand miles apart and other times only a few hours apart. We have spent years agreeing on most of the same things theologically. As I grew older, there came a point in time where I began to wrestle with some of the views handed down to me by them and others. I came out on the other side of that season with some different opinions than them. However, on some other issues we remained in agreement.

In all of the differences, we stayed together. They remained my parents. Early on in my journey of discovering other terrain to explore than that which was handed down to me through my church upbringing, I was a bit immature in how I treated those who thought differently than I did. For a season, I was a bit disrespectful to my parents and tried to push my new beliefs on them. This was not in relation to salvation, since we still agreed on the main foundations of Christianity. Rather, it was in respect to minor distinctions on certain areas of what we believed and how we did ministry. After a season, I realized that my new beliefs, while important to me, were not worth my disconnecting my heart in our relationship. There is a lot of room for diversity in the body of Christ since we all hold different parts of the Kingdom message as important. For example, the Charismatic Movement focuses heavily on the gifts of the spirit whereas some other churches may focus more on the word of God. The charismatic movement certainly values the Bible but may emphasize the Holy Spirit in a way that some other groups of believers don't. Both church types are necessary and important, but each has chosen a different level of focus given to them. This is wonderful and we need it all in the body of Christ. It is most important to realize that no matter how we differ, we still have the same Heavenly Father. Unity in the body must be our ultimate goal.

Navigating Relationships

I recall a challenging time for me when my grandfather and I started to disagree theologically. I had spent years hearing and honoring his wisdom and insights in regards to his views of the Kingdom. There came a time, however, that I started to see that some of the ways in which he viewed God were not congruent with what I believed about God. These areas were in relation to end times, God concepts, etc., and I began to think differently than him. I remember feeling awkward about having been in this relationship for so long in which we were on the same theological track to suddenly be heading a different direction. It did shift our relationship and for a bit of time, I was probably not the most gracious to him. I used to think to myself how I couldn't stand to hear him speak about certain issues that I now completely disagreed with. I didn't know how to communicate my disagreement with him, so I withdrew from that relationship and the frequentness in which we connected. Both of these relationships, with my parents and grandfather, had these moments of theological differences. However, we are still in the same kingdom, have the same Heavenly Father, but have just simply had forks in the road that left us at times in different places.

For me, learning how to keep my heart connected to them as family and Kingdom family while also honorably disagreeing was at times challenging. Now that we're all a little further along in our journeys, it's easy to walk together and we enjoy the moments that we share together. We choose not to connect around the issues that we disagree about, but rather enjoy the things that make us family. There's a lot of room for relationship regarding things that we agree on.

The same goes for a spiritual family. There has to be fathers and mothers. Obviously, we all have one Heavenly Father. He is the same Father for all of us, but our earthly spiritual fathers and mothers are various and diverse. Sometimes the relationship dynamics change with differing seasons of life. I have accepted the ebb and flow as I have moved in and out of relationships with spiritual fathers and mothers as times changed. Sometimes a relationship with a particular father was more important in one season because there was an impartation from him that I needed to receive and develop at that point in my life. After that character or development was done, our relationship shifted.

For instance, one significant fatherly voice in my life had about a five-year period of time in which he and I connected around issues of prayer, city transformation, prophetic and the nations. After that period of time, his emphasis or ministry changed and he moved to a different location. The ease in which we connected was no longer there. It was a bit disappointing for me, as I loved the connections and value of relationship that God had given me through that. However, I have grown in those matters and realize that God brings people in and out of my life for seasons to manifest a part of Himself that I may need at a given time. When this is complete, He allows them to move on and touch other people's lives. From there, I get to continue on carrying what they provided and imparted to me through that exchange of life. I always hold them in a special place in my heart, but the frequency of the relational dynamic may change.

I don't completely drop the ball in connection and communication with these individuals, because I have a high value for committed relationships. I still send a note occasionally to check in on them and see how they're doing, but it may be obvious that deeper relational interactions are no longer common. I believe this is healthy and God ordained. There may be seasons in the future that we find our paths crossing and then likewise the fire of relationship and exchange begins again. This is wonderful if that happens, but it's not necessary either.

There are other fatherly and motherly voices in our lives that seem to have more of a life-long connection. Those relationships are wonderful as well and I love the longevity of walking with family over long periods of time. They know you and you know them; there is a continual dynamic of them speaking into your life that is enriching and powerful. I am extremely grateful to have several of these long-term relationships in my life.

Sometimes, people stay in a relationship until it gets tested. The voice that was previously invited to speak into certain areas and was originally welcomed begins to agitate and irritate the person receiving the input. This person can then build a wall against the one speaking into their life and push them out. Recently, I had someone in my life that verbally declared I was their mentor, but when I started speaking into them on an issue, as a father sometimes does, they backed out and withdrew. This wasn't even a short-term relationship, but had been built over the course of time through solid interactions. I shared my heart with this person, and let him know that relationships don't always just have the warm and fuzzy feelings. But, he still chose to leave the relationship at that point.

Discipline Is a Part of Legitimate Relationships

If you want fathers and mothers in your life, sometimes there is discipline involved in the process. Discipline comes with love, but sometimes it doesn't feel good and can be a bit like getting a spanking. During those moments, you have a choice; you can be propelled into a massive breakthrough, or you can cower in defeat. If we press into relationship and look with humility at the areas that are being spoken into us, then we will find a breakthrough and will receive an inheritance not too far away from that moment.

Hebrews 12:7-9 from the Message Bible defines this process like this,

"God is educating you; that's why you must never drop out. He's treating you as dear children. This trouble you're in isn't punishment; it's training, the normal experience of children. Only irresponsible parents leave children to fend for themselves. Would you prefer an irresponsible God? We respect our own parents for training and not spoiling us, so why not embrace God's training so we can truly live?"

Elisha remained with Elijah, even though Elijah tried to get him to stop traveling with him. Elisha was tested in his personal confidence when his spiritual father kept telling him to not follow him any further. This story is shared in 2 Kings 2:6,

"Then Elijah said to him, 'Stay here; the Lord has sent me to the Jordan.' And he replied, 'As surely as the Lord lives and as you live, I will not leave you.' So the two of them walked on."

In the end, Elisha received the double portion because he persevered to the end of where God destined that relationship to go. This is revealed in 2 Kings 2:13-14,

"He picked up the cloak that had fallen from Elijah and went back and stood on the bank of the Jordan. Then he took the cloak that had fallen from him and struck the water with it. "Where now is the Lord, the God of Elijah?" he asked. When he struck the water, it divided to the right and to the left, and he crossed over."

Then Elisha had a servant, Gehazi. He stayed around with Elisha, but never really got Elisha's heart. He knew a lot of information and could recount the testimonies of Elisha's power encounters to Kings, but never received the double portion blessing that he could have had. He chose not to work on developing his character along the way to match God's heart. Maybe Elisha should have been a bit more patient with him as a father, but time can only tell. The important point to realize is that whether Elisha failed as a spiritual father or if Gehazi failed as a son, there was no transference of anointing to the next generation as was intended and needed. 2 Kings 5:26-27 relays this interaction,

"But Elisha said to him, 'Was not my spirit with you when the man got down from his chariot to meet you? Is this the time to take money, or to accept clothes, olive groves, vineyards, flocks, herds, or menservants and maidservants? Naaman's leprosy will cling to you and to your descendants forever.' Then Gehazi went from Elisha's presence and he was leprous, as white as snow."

The Key To Spiritual Inheritance

Many people stay in relationships long enough to get satisfaction and enjoyment from those they are with, but often don't stick it out through times of personal rejection or conflict to get the double portion. I have seen time and time again in my life that when I stuck it out through the disciplines that I needed, though painful, I received an inheritance on the other side. Sometimes, that inheritance came in the form of doors of influence and opportunity opening up for me. Other times I have worked with a mentor and I would receive a spiritual portion of what they carry in their anointing and gifting. That gifting and anointing came as I remained teachable and humbly receiving from how they interacted in life and ministry. This is how to receive a spiritual inheritance.

I have also had spiritual fathers that I didn't receive from. In these situations, I chose to sabotage their voices in my life because it was too painful; which then in turn stopped me from receiving a full inheritance from them. I'm sure each father needs to work at communicating more effectively and I also know that I certainly am in the process of upgrading my character to accommodate more gentleness and softness in my approach. But there does come a time when a son has to be able to remove the stumbling block of how the Father has communicated to him and receive the blessing of His voice and wisdom. The inheritance doesn't come until the lesson has been learned.

There may be many inheritances one can receive from a spiritual father or mother. We may have the privilege to journey for a long distance with one or more of the same fathers and mothers during the course of our lifetimes. What a joy that is! But either way, I am thankful for those that I have had the honor and privilege of journeying with and those that I continue to journey with now. The important point is that I perceive and welcome those that God has brought into my life to help me in this season of my journey. You may want to ask yourself whom has God currently brought into your life? Is it your boss at work, or perhaps an unbelieving Father-in law? Maybe even a pastor of a local church? Or perhaps even a stay at home mom? Could they be your home group leader? The possibilities are endless.

Whoever they are, we must have our eyes and hearts open and on the lookout for those who carry the Father's heart for us and be sensitive to create a pathway for them to speak into us. If we are to be in healthy family relationships, we have to embrace fathers and mothers and our need for them in our lives. God puts some in our lives that are near and at times some at a distance. We need those that are near because they walk with us daily, and can love us through the good, bad and ugly. Those that are far off can sometimes provide a needed voice from a distant perspective. They can also be a blessing to us when we don't have someone locally that carries what they do. However, you should not exclude local fathers at the expense of looking for someone at a distance to speak into your life.

Heroes Amongst Us

As I have traveled, I have seen that some seem to think of the traveling minister as the hero and view their local pastor/leader as an imperfect person. This is not the truth. I have been the vocational minister that stays at home and also the one that travels, and I have found that at times, the people at home can sometimes think you are the problem. When I ended my pastoral time in Willits, I had a group of folks that absolutely felt that the pastors that eventually took over after we left were wonderful. They confided in them about issues they had with my pastoring and with me personally. When I left that pastorate role to join my current team in Vacaville, those same disgruntled individuals contacted me with frustrations they now had with the new pastors who took my place. That new pastor had been their old confidant when they were frustrated with me. Now the disgruntled people desired to confide in me about their friends that were now their pastors. I gently steered them back to their local leaders. This is the perfect example of a father issue, or even an issue with authority. In those situations, it doesn't matter who the local pastor is. These types of individuals will have an issue with whoever is in the role of pastor or leader over them. As long as you are not their authority, you are acceptable in their eyes. This cycle will continue until they get healed. It's important that we all get healed so that we are connecting to fathers that are near, not just voices from a distance.

Covenant

Another marker of a healthy family is living in covenant. In a healthy biological family, there is a covenant between each of the family members. Personally, I have spent nearly forty years in constant communication with my brothers and parents. There have been many ups and downs, but we have fought together for covenant and love. Whether it is spoken or unspoken, in a true family, you know that you are in this for the long haul. It doesn't matter how many times you disagree, argue, get hurt, etc. You still come back to the Christmas table together with your biological family. Birthdays are shared, special moments and marriages are celebrated and even deaths are handled together as a family. It is a wonderful joy to be able to journey with biological family in that way. This long-term relational thinking must be translated to our spiritual families as well.

I remember a season in my life in which The Lord was teaching me about covenantal love towards another. I had been in Fiji and met an Indian taxi driver who had been in a pre-arranged marriage. He had never dated his wife nor chosen her. She was selected for him. At the point when I met him, he had been married for several years. For me, it was a strange way to get married, since in the USA, we find someone we care about, fall in love with them and then marry. I asked him how he was doing in this type of marriage arrangement. The taxi driver told me that he was so in love with her and he had an authentic giddy excitement about his wife in how he spoke about her. This really provoked me to think that maybe sometimes we choose to covenant with someone when all the right conditions seem to be present. But if love is based on conditions, then what happens when the conditions change? Maybe we need an upgraded view of being in covenant with others. We don't choose it. When we say yes to Jesus, we are saying yes to an eternal covenant with Him and His bride; our brothers and sisters. Despite the ups and downs of emotions and the excitement and at times pain of being together, we choose to stay connected in love.

It is wonderful to find people as we go along in life that we share that sense of covenant with. It is also wonderful to have friends that move into the family category in our lives. Family is a higher level of covenant and more enduring than friendship. When you find people who have stood the test of time in your life, despite how many times you move, change vocations, move in and out of relationships, succeed and fail; they are there with you. There is a covenant, whether spoken or unspoken, formal or informal. This is what we need in the kingdom and it is worth fighting for.

Unfortunately, in the church arena, there is as much divorce within the church as there is outside the church. This same spirit dwells in people that continue to wander from church to church regarding "issues" with the people or leaders at their present church. In these situations, there is a lack of covenantal understanding. Some people leave properly and others leave poorly. I have heard many reasons why people left; theological differences, hurt feelings, disagreements, unmet expectations, offense, etc. The list is endless. I do realize that at times, you need to move from one body to another based on guidance from the Lord. Sometimes it is strategic and necessary for the sake of the Kingdom and God provides us with the wisdom and insight to move to other locations as needed. But if we feel that it's time to leave, we need to be sure we are planning to leave for the right reasons as well as that we are staying for the right reasons.

God's Big Family

My wife Heather and I pastored for 10 years in Willits, CA. While we were there, we found such love and a sense of family amongst our body. The Lord had spoken during those years that there would come a time when we would move to another location that would better facilitate the dreams of our hearts. When that time came in 2008, we moved to Vacaville where we have now lived for the last 6 years. Our hearts are still knitted in love towards those at our home in Willits and no one can take away the special care and love for those we have there. In fact, periodically we visit there and speak into the life of the congregation. We also connect with the current pastors and leaders so that we can maintain relationships when we are invited to do so. We realize that times have changed and things don't look the same, but we still recognize that they were more than a congregation to us; they were our family. They are and always will be dear to our hearts, as we have had many wonderful memories together.

However, as previously mentioned, God moved us to Vacaville so that our dreams could continue to unfold. As we have journeyed towards our dreams we have spent time developing that same sense of family. We have not replaced our Willits family that we cherished, but we have found fulfillment with our local church family. Our hearts found covenant with our Willits family and that will never be broken, but we have also had to fight to find covenant with our Vacaville family.

Covenant is challenging in the church world. In a biological family, you choose to come together year in and year out, through good and bad. You find a way to weather the storms of life and continually stay together. Sometimes a divorce pulls apart someone that was a member of the biological family and our heart disconnects with the one that is not in our immediate family of brothers and sisters. This is really sad and not the heart of God. Sometimes also in the church world, a person's heart disconnects with the local church and becomes stone cold to it. They can then build a case against their church and before too long, they have moved on elsewhere. I don't believe that this is the way God intended for believers to do church. I believe that there are times when we need to move to another location because God is doing something in us that only that other place can bring. It is critical to line up our purpose, people and place to have success. This is a great message that David Crone has helped us discover over and over again at the Mission in Vacaville. We covenant with people we have purpose with, who we feel that sense of family with, and where the location fits what is in our hearts. If those values change, sometimes God is shifting our location or changing the people we relate to.

It is always disappointing to see people beginning to connect with other people who are disgruntled. It is one thing to connect in purpose with others, but it is entirely another to let your heart grow bitter and resentful together. This can then lead to other connections with disconnected people around a festering wound. These types of relationships never end well. It's always best to choose healthy covenant. In covenant, the highs and lows of the relationship don't matter. Disagreements and misunderstandings don't separate, but are just part of the relationship. The covenant is always important.

In my personal journey with my wife, we have had to fight to keep our hearts for those that we serve and work with. We have had seasons where we had to call each other up to a higher point of finding the gold in our local body instead of pointing to what we felt needed fixing. We have had to fight to protect our hearts from becoming disconnected from those we are with since we know that any seed of bitterness, frustration or unmet expectations not dealt with will eventually cause us to be disqualified from what God is offering us here in this covenant. When you are in covenant, you are committed to working things out no matter what. You are committed to honoring others, even and especially during disagreement. You are committed to valuing and supporting what others are doing even if it doesn't seem to directly benefit you. Serving others demonstrates that we do love them and this is not just about doing ministry, but also about loving others and demonstrating that by helping them succeed in their heart dreams.

You may want to ask yourself some questions about covenant. Whom are you serving? Where are you sowing? Are you keeping your heart pure and clean from any bitterness? When someone comes to you about a problem they have with your friends, church leaders, brothers in Christ, etc., how do you handle that? I recall recently talking with a friend who asked me what I thought about another minister we both know. I knew my friend had an issue with him, but I didn't want to empower the disagreement by partnering with his issue towards this minister. I actually had some of the same issues as he did, but I decided that I would honor and speak highly of our friend. As soon as I did that, the conversation came up to a higher and healthier place. It could have easily spiraled downward into negativity and criticism towards our brother in Christ.

Later on, The Lord shared with me that my choice to not agree with this corrupt communication actually helped my friend see this fellow brother from a better perspective. Another question to ask yourself and consider is: Are we working hard at protecting covenants we have with other believers? We know we may disagree, but in family, you know you will remain together and nothing will ever change that. Being in a healthy family requires that you continue to choose the things that build healthy relationships and covenant so that no distance is created. If we are going to reform to become family, we will have to tether ourselves to covenant in a world that doesn't fight for covenant.

Living in Community

Another core value that we must uphold is the value of living in community. In America, we have a high value for independence. There is certainly strength in pursuing personal purpose and dreams, but there is also an unhealthy danger if that core value is not built within the culture of community. Individual dreams are better fulfilled in the context of community. There is a common cause that brings us together and we rally around people that carry similar values and causes.

We develop cultures of community around our work. What draws us together? The fact that we work at the same job together. Sometimes we rally around sports or a favorite team. We are meant to find community within even larger community contexts. It is a part of the value of common purpose and people. You gather together with people that you enjoy, but they are also heading towards a common purpose and/or goal. In our local church, we have people that gather around worship, but within that worship community there are sub-communities such as song writing, worship leading, etc.

Some churches are small enough that your community includes those that you meet with weekly for worship and connecting with

God. I remember the joy of pastoring Shiloh in Willits for 10 years. It was awesome to connect relationally in a small church of 50 - 100 people. The kinds of connections that we developed in that place are precious, deep and life changing. In the smaller settings like this, life is shared during times of meals and general fellowship. It is important to remember that we must always share life together and are not meant to build life on our own. We need a group of people to do life together with. Whether we belong to a larger or smaller church, we can still find a smaller group of people to build connections with.

It is important to remain tethered to someone else outside of us. The communities of people that we connect with can change our dreams, purposes and calls. In these communities, we find those that we spend more time with become brothers, sisters, friends and life partners. This is all a part of creating family. If you are not in community with people around a common purpose and pursuit, then you will not stay in a local church for very long. Some people just like going to church to hear a good word, but their lives are disconnected from people. The problem with this is that we were not created independently of each other.

Cain complained to God when God asked him where his brother Abel was in Genesis 4:9,

> "Then the Lord said to Cain, 'Where is your brother Abel?'
> 'I don't know,' he replied. 'Am I my brother's keeper?'"

The best answer would have been yes. I am my brother's keeper. We are responsible for each other. We are not on our own. Perhaps our larger world has taught us independence and self-sustenance, but that value in and of itself is not a healthy value to live by.

As I have traveled outside the US, I have noticed that sometimes other cultures have more of a community mindset. Their goals are to protect the greater good for everyone, not just themselves. In our attempt to empower individuals and break away from mindlessly following a corporate vision, we may have lost a precious jewel that was there. We must be tied and held together by a sense of community and a set of values. Acts 2:42-44 demonstrates the way community functioned in the early church,

> "They devoted themselves to the apostles' teaching and to the fellowship, to the breaking of bread and to prayer. Everyone was filled with awe, and many wonders and miraculous signs were done by the apostles. All the believers were together and had everything in common. Selling their possessions and goods, they gave to anyone as he had need."

The early church had a set of beliefs that caused them to find purpose together. They also enjoyed one another and had a sense of common purpose that caused them to share life together. They gave their possessions to those in need regardless of the level of relationship. Today, we need a breakthrough like this in our church. We work towards sharing when it is convenient and not painful. In the family context, a father would sacrifice much to help his children advance. Also, a family would do whatever they could to help each other get food on the table, and meet basic needs if it came to that. You cannot expect a body of believers to function as an extremely generous community without first establishing a strong sense of family ties. Until we begin to truly think like family, we will not see the benefits of family unleashed. Extreme generosity would be the fruit of strong family bonds. In a healthy community, everyone truly cares for each other since there is a larger common purpose that all are working towards.

The financial curse over our lands will be broken as we turn our hearts to relationships. Malachi 4:6 relays it this way, "He will turn the hearts of the fathers to their children, and the hearts of the children to their fathers; or else I will come and strike the land with a curse." I wonder if some of our financial breakthroughs are connected to this truth? We must realize that in the body of believers we are connected with, each one of us are in a local community family. I say local because it is not practical to meet the needs of every believer on the planet. It seems that more often than not, our community needs should be met within a more local setting and then we can reach outside the community for connections as time allows.

Do you have a community that you are connected to? Are they healthy or disgruntled? Do you have people in community that you are partnered with to advance your dreams? Are you helping others fulfill their dreams? Do you help serve people when there is no personal reward? Because serving is what family does for each other. Do you see your community as family or as a place to function with for only a season? Are your relationships need driven or covenant driven? Or, in other words, are you only connected for what you are receiving or are you connected because you belong?

The markers of having fathers, covenant and community are just a few that I feel can guide us in creating cultures of family amongst believers. In the next chapter, I will further delve into some of the markers we are looking for in fathers and mothers. Each of us are called to manifest the Father's heart to those around us and understanding that will give us greater clarity regarding what we should pursue.

Chapter 8

Characteristics Of Fathers

In this concluding chapter, we will explore characteristics that a spiritual father exhibits. These characteristics are values that men and women can embrace and manifest. The heart of the Father is carried through both men and women, and is not gender specific. If we want the ministry of the Father to be restored to this earth as a primary ministry, then we must focus on this area. As we get a clearer picture of our Heavenly Father, then sustainable fatherly characteristics that we want to embody will become more evident. The only characteristics that can truly evoke a change in people are those that come from heaven. So let's explore some characteristics of the Father that we should be manifesting and modeling to others.

An Upgrade in Gentleness

Gentleness is an attribute of the emerging fathers that will become more common. I love the strength of fathers in the faith that have been tested and have weathered the storms of life, but it is the gentleness of a strong father that can break condemnation, performance and ultimately produce life. The Lord told me months ago that I needed to emphasize the fruit of patience, gentleness and kindness in my life during this next season.

While I was undergoing my upgrade into gentleness in the last season, I noticed that I tended to be very impatient. Impatience produces a lack of gentleness. Simple things, such as rushing from one location to another, causes me to get angry at people that are driving slowly in front of me, or cashiers that take a long time to check my groceries out. I have noticed that when I intentionally slow down, it creates gentleness in and of itself. I begin to think more clearly and my thoughts turn to patience and kindness. I may feel like it's important to get somewhere in a hurry. As I slow down, I realize that I may be a bit late but it is not the end of the world. Sometimes we fear being late because we don't want to be punished for not being prompt. Not only that, but timeliness and promptness are highly valued in the part of the country I live in, so this is naturally a part of the culture around me. I value time and being on time, but sometimes things just happen that can prevent you from being on time. This entire mindset can steal gentleness, since Matthew 11:29-30 says,

"Take my yoke upon you and learn from me, for I am gentle and humble in heart, and you will find rest for your souls. For my yoke is easy and my burden is light."

Since we have Jesus in us, we may have to slow down to actually realize that He is gentle. He is not in a hurry, even though He is intentional about what He is doing. Impatience can sabotage our blessing. I have found that when I am impatient, a number of other ungodly characteristics flow from me that don't represent the Father to others. Moses was kept out of the Promised Land for his anger. Saul's kingship was turned over to David because his fear of man caused him to offer a sacrifice that he was supposed to wait upon Samuel for. It was his impatience out of the fear of man that disqualified him. This is demonstrated in the scriptures below:

1 Samuel 13:11-12, "'What have you done?' asked Samuel. Saul replied, 'When I saw that the men were scattering, and that you did not come at the set time, and that the Philistines were assembling at Micmash, I thought, *'Now the Philistines will*

come down against me at Gilgal, and I have not sought the Lord's favor.' So I felt compelled to offer the burnt offering.'"

1 Samuel 13:13-14 "'You acted foolishly,' Samuel said. 'You have not kept the command the Lord your God gave you; if you had, he would have established your kingdom over Israel for all time. But now your kingdom will not endure; the Lord has sought out a man after his own heart and appointed him leader of his people, because you have not kept the Lord's command.'

For many years, my view of Jesus has been the warrior Jesus; one with fiery eyes, a sword protruding from His mouth with strength. My thoughts were to not mess with this Jesus since He is in charge. This came from the picture I saw in Revelation 1, but sometimes we need an upgrade of what we think those pictures really represent. Even though He is the strong and powerful Jesus, He is also the gentle and kind Jesus. I love how Song of Solomon 5:12-13 in the message Bible describes His eyes and face,

"His eyes are like doves, soft and bright,
but deep-set, brimming with meaning, like wells of water.
His face is rugged, his beard smells like sage,
His voice, his words, warm and reassuring."

As I have spent time with Him in this last season and looked into those eyes in my spirit, I realize how soft and tender they are. They really are eyes of fire, but gentle. Matthew 12:20 says about His character,

"A bruised reed he will not break,
and a smoldering wick he will not snuff out,
till he leads justice to victory."

He is so careful around those that are broken and tender with those that are bruised. He is so patient with those who take awhile accepting His incredible love. How forgiving He is to those struggling in sin. I used to think that Jesus was kind during the crucifixion, but after He resurrected, watch out! Jesus in fact was operating in extreme kindness as He was being crucified. He did not fight back, He didn't return accusations, and he didn't defend Himself even though He had the authority to call upon many angels to rescue Him. But then I also used to think that after His resurrection, His focus was power. Don't mess with Him now, He won't put up with it. Then I realized that yes, He is powerful, but He is also still gentle. He was modeling His very nature when He died on the cross. When He told us to turn the other cheek in scripture, that was not a passing principle. It was a value of Heaven. Matthew 5:39, "But I tell you, Do not resist an evil person. If someone strikes you on the right cheek, turn to him the other also."

A while back, the Lord had me go on a fast from certain adventurous and more violent movies. My appetite for violent and revengeful movies had been greatly reduced over the last years, but I still sensed the Lord was inviting me into another level of sensitivity with Him. I admit that I struggled for a few days to decide whether or not to take Him up on this offer. When I finally said yes, and began the fast, I noticed a wonderful increase of sensitivity to His presence. Revelation began to flow and a fresh sense of the Father's heart began to visit me. I found that my heart was being weeded of what is absent in heaven, and new, beautiful things were being planted in their place. This time, it didn't come with the condemnation I felt in years past about having to rid myself of all earthly things, such as movies. I didn't feel the Lord's displeasure if I decided to watch something. Rather, it was an invitation that was so subtle, yet so rewarding. Additionally, the increase of quality time with my family was very fruitful and provided us an open avenue in which to engage with each other separate from media. I actually didn't realize how much of a rut we had fallen into. All of this allowed the more gentle side of me to emerge as I allowed my mind and heart to be washed from the subtle desensitizing of my spirit to vengeful things. Jesus really is so kind and His heart loves everyone. I found that as I became more sensitive to the gentle Jesus, his still small voice, and the quiet and kind approach of God, I actually began to publicly communicate more gently as well. I also was not so sharp in dealing with correction and found myself handling others more gracefully.

Leadership Lessons

Do you manifest gentleness towards those that try your patience or you are frustrated with? At times, I have brought down a strong correction towards those that I was in long-term relationship with and noticed that it more often severed the relationship instead of built it. I learned a valuable lesson in this area during this last season. I sense and know when God wants to bring a change in an area of people's lives, and have thus gone after it when I preach. I spent months going after one issue in particular within our youth group. As time went on, I noticed their lack of fully embracing the message I preached was causing my communication of that message to get harsher. I continued to hammer the same message, until finally I remembered a time when I had pastored in Willits for 10 years. I had the same sharpness in preaching to the people there as well, when some didn't seem to change. I had preached about character development to no avail, and this created a tension and frustration in me that caused me to lose my kindness and gentleness. Remembering Willits helped me recognize that I didn't want to carry that same harshness in my heart towards our youth. This helped me to release the issues I had been going after. I took a break from preaching on those issues and realized that others and myself had planted many seeds of God's word into the youth, so it was time to let those seeds grow. I noticed an immediate release from tension in that area and was able to step back and approach the youth from a kinder and gentler position.

I have also noticed this same thing happens with my own children. The more I look at the issue I want to see changed in them, the more frustrated I get. Especially if I don't perceive that they are changing fast enough or if I see a pattern of repeated misbehavior. I decided to side with loving them and letting them personally face the consequences for their lack of character development in an area of growth instead of forcing my wisdom upon them. I was able to step into a happier mindset instead of continually being agitated and frustrated with them. My children were also much more at ease with this approach as well.

You may want to ask yourself some questions about this. Are there areas in others that you get frustrated with? Are there issues you have been dealing with for some time that do not yet seem to be at a breakthrough point? Are there things you want to see done in the Kingdom in the lives of those around you? Are you patiently planting the seeds in them, looking for those that are growing, while blessing those that chosoe not to? All of these things help us maintain and nurture a spirit of gentleness as people slowly develop; sometimes slower than we would hope.

Patient Dad

In addition to gentleness, the nature of a father manifests incredible patience. They both seem to go together hand in hand. We are all called to manifest the Father to those around us. We all are modeling whatever Father view is most prevalent in our thinking.

I remember specifically deciding to discipline someone intentionally in a way that I had been disciplined. This method didn't really produce great fruit in me personally and after I had done it, I remember asking myself "Do I really want to model my discipline of others after the way I was disciplined?" Sometimes we don't even realize it, but the way in which people we esteem have modeled behaviors to us can become validated by us.

Recently, I had this revelation in my parenting. My son wanted to go fishing, hunting and camping - boy stuff. I had done some of that when I was a kid, but I don't really remember my parents being into those activities. It just wasn't their thing. When my son asked me to go, I thought to myself "that's not really what I do because I never really did that growing up." It sounds like a silly thought, but it was real. I then had another thought "just because my parents never did that with me does not mean that I can't learn another way for my son. Maybe I can learn to do some of those things with my son and create a new path for my family in that area." Sometimes we don't realize that we have picked up things we embrace or that we don't embrace, do's and don'ts because it was handed to us.

We must have the courage to ask ourselves some real questions about this. Do I want to continue this? Is the way that I was taught to manage relationships the healthiest way? Do I want to discipline those around me the way in which I was disciplined? Do I want to carry on every behavior that my natural parents or spiritual parents modeled to me?

We are all imperfect in how we model Heavenly Father to others. We have glimpses of Him that cause us to respond to others accordingly, but we also need each other to help shed a more complete light on Him. I want the gentleness of others to rub off on me. I want the kindness, patience, compassion, self-control and the love for the unlovely to rub off on me. I want the glimpses of the Father I have seen and I am modeling to also rub off on others.

Beyond Roles, Titles and Labels

Our role is to see who the Father is and what He is doing, and then to model that. We have to tap into His heart for others if we want to truly influence others with heaven. We should ask ourselves do I exude patience to others who are friends, family, children, fathers, mothers, co-workers, pastors, leaders, and people of influence or people in trouble? The other day, I was getting my car repaired. I had purchased a warranty when I originally bought the car and was rather happy that I had. However, I didn't notice until I took the car in for service that there was a deductible that I would need to pay every time the warranty was used. I didn't remember the car sales person covering this specifically with me, and I was upset about it. I had worked hard to get this warranty included in the purchase and my first thought at this point was to think negatively of car salespeople. Specifically I thought "Those car salesman are all the same, all they are thinking of is taking advantage of you for their own good." At this point, it wasn't too long before I heard the Father say to me "Keith, those aren't car salesman. They are people." He instantly elevated me into a much kinder and more patient frame of mind. I repented and thanked the Lord for these good people.

How often do we find ourselves placing people into categories? Those government people, those pastors, those rich folks, etc. We can all do it if we are not careful. The Lord sees them all as His people. He shared with me "Keith, just like you have been a third generation vocational minister, so have many of those in government or business had generational connection to that arena. You understand your world, and they understand theirs. They are not bad people with bad motives, but rather they are simply people doing the best they can in the sphere of influence they are a part of."

I have noticed that whenever we get impatient with people, often times it is because we don't or haven't taken the time to understand them. I find that the more I understand why someone is the way they are, the more compassion, love, patience, etc. that I have for them. Sometimes I may be agitated with someone, maybe even my own child. Let's say they are not acting properly - they are a bit grumpy, disrespectful, or mouthy. I don't tolerate disrespect, so I punish it. Later on, I find out that they had a rough day. Something happened that hurt them. When I took time to care for them and listen to their day, then I gained understanding for them. When they feel understood and are able to get free of the hurts from their day, then their respect for their surroundings and me automatically grows. If I come down hard on them, then I lose the connection I could have gained by taking a little more time to find out what was really driving their bad behavior.

I wonder how many people we have misread, misjudged or not been patient with only to find out later that what they were going through was driving their bad behavior? If we could get a bit of a bigger picture of the people around us, the circumstances we are in, what is going on in our church and our local community gatherings, we may see something totally different. If we could find ourselves stretching time out, looking down the road a few years, peering into God's view at all the circumstances that are happening to us and those around us, then we may have a different view. Some of the things we may think are wrong may not be so devastating and dramatic to us in light of the broader picture. Sometimes we look at what is going on in people's lives and don't get the broader picture of what God is doing with them, and then we can mistakenly judge them. What we may not realize is that perhaps they have a long history we don't understand as well as a wonderful future that all things can be redeemed within. A great spiritual father in the faith once told me that the best thing I can do for my children when they are not behaving appropriately is to love them. He also said that in the long run, they will think I am a genius for doing that. We can apply this same guidance to others that we are fathering. Find ways to care for them and fill up their love tanks, then all the issues that seem so big right now will seem so small in the future.

Manifesting The Father

To some, we are the only model of the Heavenly Father they may ever see. What are we modeling? Many times we are a part of what God is using to model His heart to them. What characteristics of the Father do you personally carry? What is He trying to develop in you to more fully manifest His heart to those around you? Who has He placed in your life to grow you in that fruit? Sometimes we are so agitated with those He has placed in our lives that seem to push up against us, but we fail to realize they may be the very vehicle God is using to cause a certain fruit of the Father to come forth in our lives. All of the fruits are found in Christ, who lives in us. But some of the fruits haven't been seen through us because we haven't yet yielded that part of our lives to Him. If we could see that a difficult person or situation in our lives is a helpful tool to accelerate us to the next level, maybe we would embrace the journey and process instead of resisting the whole way. When we learn to fully embrace what the Father is doing, we find that our journey of growth in that area is quicker and others more easily see that fruit in our lives.

God wants us to bear fruit and fruit is born as we reveal Christ. Christ revealed the Father and the Father was revealed through Christ. We have been given the nature of God because we have Christ in us as a gift. How we nurture that gift in our daily encounters with God is what causes us to manifest His fruit in our lives. Spending time with Jesus is a must to continue to carry the heavenly heart of the Father to those around us. I find that when I spend time with Jesus, I am much more enjoyable to be around. I have a much more caring heart for those that are around me. I exhibit more patience, kindness and gentleness. I am also more generous and giving. When I don't take time to be with Him, it's not too long before I become agitated, irritated, and angry, and before too long I have gotten myself into a mess. If we are to see the church truly move from a house to a home, we must continue to do what Jesus did. Get alone to be with the Father. That's what family is about anyways. Being with fathers, mothers, sisters and brothers. It is such a joy to see how much of the atmosphere of heaven's family we can get here on the earth.

Developing Wisdom to Inherit

Fathers also carry the heart to see sons and daughters come into their inheritance. You must have the characteristics of gentleness and patience to help them get there. Sons and daughters can upset fathers and mothers at times. I know that all too well from my own children. Sometimes they slap my back in frustration or do something irresponsible that I warned them many times not to do. Those situations can cause me to lose my cool if I let them. I can also turn their wrong behaviors into right behaviors, as I walk in healthy character. My goal as a father is to turn over more responsibility to them. I want them to walk in the full privileges of being in my house. My job as a parent is to prepare them to be fully responsible in life. I am also called to demonstrate unconditional love to them, which includes establishing in them who they are and helping them discover what they are going to do in life. Ultimately, I want them to be able to handle all the privileges of life without sabotaging themselves.

I have been in the development process with one of my children in the area of building trust over the last several years. They have both had to spend months at a time building trust with me. As their trust grows, they get more privileges. In order to get more privileges, they have to become more responsible, trustworthy and more understanding of my heart in that matter. They then have to successfully walk out their understanding of what I have been training them in if they are to enjoy the freedom they desire in an area. Both of my children have their own cell phones and access to media such as Facebook, e-mail and a variety of other apps. Demonstrating their understanding of what we require as parents will cause them to get more or less of these privileges. One of them took longer than the other choosing to continually push the boundaries, hide things, lie, while at the same time trying to convince me that they are ready for full privileges. I let them know they can have as much or as little of these privileges when they have demonstrated their ability to protect what I am looking for. It has been a challenging walk for both of us in the journey of building trust together. I have wracked my head up against the wall many times trying to understand why they wouldn't just simply choose to walk within the set guidelines. The other child has learned how to be trustworthy in this area. It took this one a year or so to learn how to protect daddy's heart in this, but they now do. When they have fallen short or not honored the heart we have for those things, they have come openly to confess their shortcomings. In doing so, they continue to enjoy the freedom that is being offered because of their trustworthiness.

My heart as a dad in all of this is that they get to come to a place of inheritance. I want to give them the farm, so to speak; but I want to make sure they don't burn it down first. They need to feel appreciated and valued, while also stewarding the gifts, blessings, privileges and inheritances they receive along the way. I don't want to continually have my children rely on me to determine what freedoms they can enjoy. I want them to get to the point that they are self-sufficient and mature in that area. It is my joy to give over to them certain things when I know they are responsible enough to handle them.

A parent who is going to give his child a car or let him drive the family car should make sure they are capable of taking care of the car before they are given this privilege. In other areas, I have made the mistake of giving out more privilege before trust was built. Time and time again, my child has proven they are not trustworthy by how they behave in a certain situation. This has shown me that my job as a parent must not extend that level of freedom until they are able to manage it. I want to give them things that will be a blessing to them and not destroy them. The prodigal son took the inheritance of the Father and went out and squandered it in loose living. He didn't understand the heart of the Father in what that blessing was intended for.

Going the Distance

Fathers and mothers are those who want to give blessings to the sons and daughters that have learned to protect their parent's hearts.

The hearts of a father and mother are not controlling, impure, or for selfish gain. A true parent's goal is that their child's success be sustainable. I love the fathers and mothers that God has brought into my life that have fought hard to ensure that I would be able to handle the success of all the prophetic promises God has given me. One of my spiritual fathers shared with me that I would be able to go the distance, be able to handle success and not fail because I had invited fathers into every area of my life. Fathers that are welcomed into spiritual children's lives are capable of bringing them to a point of success. That success is always determined by how willing the child is to embrace the changes needed. Fathers long to give part of their personal influence, gifts, blessings and open doors to the sons and daughters they know are ready for it.

Another attribute of spiritual fathers is the heart to nurture, shape, and help the son or daughter discover his or her identity. A father takes the time to get to know the ones entrusted to him. They realize that their words are so powerful and can help the sons and daughters transition from a place of insecurity to security in who they are. Only Fathers that are truly secure in who they are themselves, can truly speak identity into the sons. Sons that embrace the identity spoken into them will end up becoming successful. It takes a secure father to make a successful son or daughter. I so enjoy it when my children outdo me in something. They outdo me because they have received from me and now are increasing what they received.

Cross-Cultural Parenting

Some of those that I have had the honor to speak life into are the Fijians. My wife and I had the privilege of planting a supernatural school there a few years ago. We taught them many things, and some of those things were concepts they had never walked in. Healing, prophecy, power, presence, hearing from God, etc. were all foreign concepts. Going back after a few years, it was such a joy to discover how far they had progressed in those areas. A few years later, I led a team of 30 people from the states over to be with our Fijian students in a distant island from the mainland of Fiji. We were to be holding some meetings together that night and I had our students from Fiji, who were now leading supernatural schools on their own, open the meetings. They flowed in power, created a heavenly atmosphere, prophesied at high levels and walked in many other things we had taught them. Joyfully and with contentment in my heart, I knew that my job there was done. They were not only walking in the things we had taught them, but they were actually carrying them further than we had gone with them. They were seeing many more miracles, larger miracles, more prophetic fire and more breakthroughs on the streets. My heart was filled with joy as I saw their success.

I remember previous years with them. We took time to speak into them who they were. Some of the women were beaten down, insecure and behind the scenes. The culture in Fiji at that time wasn't conducive to women in ministry or preaching. As we began to speak their identity into them, telling them how powerful they are, calling their dreams and gifts forth, they began to step into them. Now, some of them are running powerful ministries and have found success in a variety of areas. It was a struggle at first, but as we were able to encourage them, they have come forth.

One of our ladies, Maggie, has a strong prophetic mantle on her. Her mantle is as a prophetic teacher. She had declared over herself that she wanted to be the first Fijian woman to preach on the prophetic. Several years and many encouraging words later, we were privileged to go on a boat with her to an island where she taught her first prophetic training. Now she trains in a variety of areas and is walking in her destiny. Her inheritance is secure and her identity has been established. That is the absolute joy of my heart to see people come into who they are. Fathers help sons and daughters become secure in who they are.

Recognizing Fatherly Traits

I would like to close this chapter and book by mentioning some additional characteristics and attributes of fathers. Fathers create a loving atmosphere of accountability where breakthrough in areas needing development can be realized. Fathers are available and accessible to nurture sons and daughters. Fathers bring loving correction and direction. Fathers are fun. Fathers are encouragers of the sons and daughters' dreams. Fathers create platforms and open doors for dreams to come to pass. Fathers love unconditionally. Fathers are good at kick starting or creating momentum for the sons and daughters that may have gotten stuck in an area. Fathers nurture gifts. Fathers make room for the next generation to rise. Fathers help sons and daughters learn how to create winning relationships. Fathers nurture a safe environment where the sons and daughters can be vulnerable. Fathers sow resources into the sons and daughters to help ensure their success. Fathers are good listeners.

These are just some of the characteristics of the fathers that we know of today. Each of these attributes of a father are needed to see a healthy culture created in the church. If we are going to move the house of God to a home, we are going to need fathers and mothers in mass that know how to walk in the culture of our heavenly home. I believe there is a generation of sons and daughters who will rise up to be the fathers and mothers so that a harvest will be sustainable.

A New Day

What an exciting day we live in where we can each be a part of creating the new forms of a culture that will be a part of the emerging church for years to come. I pray that grace be released to you that will enable you to become the son or daughter and father or mother you are called to be, so that God can entrust you with the harvest he wants you to have. I pray that you will have courage right now to step into the place in the family God has called you to be in. Fathers and mothers are so needed and I am crying out that God will raise up many who will give themselves to making the church a home. May you be a part of the reformation that is upon us. Help make the house of God a home. God bless you.

Keith

Keith B. Ferrante

2014 Reformation Prophecy

Below is the prophetic word that the Lord gave me in the year 2014. I leave it with you because it was what compelled me to write this book. It defines a bit of what the reformation will look like as well as provides benchmarks for us all to reach for.

2014 - The Year the Reformation Begins

This is the year in which the reforming of the church will be visible and tangible. I believe the following are some of the keys to the change:

1. **Living a lifestyle of sincere vulnerability will reveal fresh life. Doubt will be removed and peoples' hope in God will be restored again. 1 Kings 17 is a major reference point for this.**

1 Kings 17:17-24, "Some time later the son of the woman who owned the house became ill. He grew worse and worse, and finally stopped breathing. She said to Elijah, 'What do you have against me, man of God? Did you come to remind me of my sin and kill my son?'
'Give me your son,' Elijah replied. He took him from her arms, carried him to the upper room where he was staying, and laid him on his bed. Then he cried out to the Lord, 'O Lord my God, have you brought tragedy also upon this widow I am staying with, by causing her son to die?' Then he stretched himself out on the boy three times and cried to the Lord, 'O Lord my God, let this boy's life return to him!' The Lord heard Elijah's cry, and the boy's life returned to him, and he lived. Elijah picked up the child and carried him down from the room into the house. He gave him to his mother and said, 'Look, your

son is alive!' Then the woman said to Elijah, 'Now I know that you are a man of God and that the word of the Lord from your mouth is the truth.'"

It will take many fathers and mothers in the faith to lie on the dead sons and daughters to restore life. This action is a reflection of the vulnerability and openness needed in order to revive life in those that have lost life, hope, purpose, purity and a future. Fathers and mothers who share life with openness and authenticity will have greater favor and influence this year and will begin to truly create family. Church venues that catch this heartbeat will experience a change in their meetings. They will become more like a living room experience with healthy family gatherings. Out of those times, and in those settings, lives will be transformed. Sons and daughters will start to come home in this atmosphere. Once the word gets out that there's safety at home, then many will flood to those places that have created home.

2. Church will begin to look and feel more like a family.

Many church leaders will begin to explore options within the church service context from which to create more intimacy and a family setting. This will then create a safe environment for hidden sins or issues to come out so people can be healed. In addition, there will be a transition from preaching as the main emphasis to modeling family with true fathers and mothers sharing their lives freely.

3. Perseverance will be key in this time.

Fathers and mothers will need to continue to open themselves up mouth-to-mouth, eye-to-eye and body-to-body with the children of God to see breakthrough. When vulnerability has persevered, then the children of God will begin to let their guards down and allow the deep places of their hearts to be seen.

4. We must obtain freedom ourselves so that we can lead others into freedom.

We cannot help others out of issues until we are completely free in those areas ourselves. We can't speak change into people if we haven't allowed change to take place in us fully and we cannot talk about the need to be completely honest if we aren't. We can't expect breakthrough from addictions to things of darkness if we are taking part in that darkness ourselves. Jesus addressed this when He said anger is of the same spirit as murder. He also said lust is the same as committing adultery as referenced in Matthew 5. Our authority will need to come from a true place of purity and light. More power will be released when we have experienced consistency in these areas.

5. We must truly get to know the King so that our power has authority and authenticity behind it.

In Acts 19 the sons of Sceva were found not carrying genuine power and were beat up by the demonic. We can't let this happen to us. In Judges 16, Samson's impurities and compromises eventually cost him his power. We must learn from this and set ourselves free from hiddenness and compromise so that a greater and more sustainable power will flow through us, not giving the enemy an internal point of access. Darkness will have greater influence on those who have allowed darkness in, but those who have embraced the light will have greater Kingdom influence with more peace. All sustainable light comes from the revelation that we are co-crucified, co-buried, co-risen and co-seated with Christ at the right hand of God. By the grace of God, we are now children of light and must eliminate anything from our lives that is not a part of our heavenly man. Reference Ephesians 5:8-12.

6. Worship will release the lightings of God as described in 2 Chronicles 20.

In this scripture, halal praise released confusion over the enemy's camp, which caused the enemy's defeat and ultimate victory for the people of God. One definition of halal praise is to flash forth light. 2 Chronicles 20:25 relays that when we are truly walking as sons and daughters of the Father of lights, our praise will flash forth light that will route the darkness and bring in great tangible spoils. Praise services will carry power when backed by people of purity who have embraced the one in them that is light.

7. Two major issues that are being removed from the body right now are bitterness and sexual immorality.

There are many offshoots to these and God is in the process of cleaning out every little inroad these may have in our lives. Many have embraced some level of these sins in smaller forms, but when they grow and manifest into the full form, the unfortunate consequence of that is spiritual death. Romans 6:23 reflects this truth. God is eliminating every bit of unforgiveness, judgments toward others, pride, prejudice, hate, hurt, impurity, compromise in what we look at, who we look at, and what we desire. These areas allow access for the enemy to steal our inheritance as described in Hebrews 12:15-17.

8. Fathers and mothers who have learned to walk free of these things will help many others obtain freedom so that blessings can be poured out again.

In humility, we must restore those who have been tainted by these sins. As we create a place of acceptance that leads to repentance from these sins and unhealthy mindsets, we will see a great harvest of souls flood into the family of Christ.

9. Just as the prodigal's father had to run towards the son and hug him, it will take fathers loving and holding sons and daughters, removing the shame and clothing them with new identity to see the children rise. Luke 15 is our reference point for this.

We must remove the unclean identities from the sons and daughters that have been acquired by the world and replace them with garments of truth, light, love, humility and heavenly identity. This is our primary job - to raise up people who carry this same heart. The emphasis must remain on being a vulnerable and approachable father or mother who doesn't need the title, but walks in the grace of the Heavenly Father to those all around them. Whether people we encounter are friends, family, fathers, sons or daughters in each of these relationships we need to manifest the heart of the Father. All forms of the five-fold ministry and the ministry of the saints must come from this place as well.

10. Some characteristics of true fathers and mothers include being approachable, identity givers, lovers, and protectors who look after the children in a caring, tender and compassionate manner.

Fathers and mothers must be firm when necessary against any enemies that steal purity, but tender and gentle towards those they nurture. A consistence in relationship with sons and daughters must come from any and all who carry the Father's heart, not just from the paid vocational pastors. They must continue in being accessible and available to create sustainable freedom. Of course, once a person takes advantage of this privilege, then they must be prepared to share wisdom at just the right time.

11. The wow factor many still have for the platform and the pulpit must be diminished and ultimately eliminated.

A growing understanding of the ministry that reconciles people should grow in the place of platform need. Whether it's public or private, the ministry of reconciliation must become our focus. The platform and pulpit are still necessary and important, but the leaders that are on stage are not there for personal gain. There has to be a role model of how church looks, even in our building set-ups if we are going to see the reformation that brings great harvest. Every era can be identified in the buildings or gathering places that developed during each one. The high buildings with great architecture and distant podiums displayed a view of God as majestic that was preached some time ago. We still see God as majestic, but what is He unveiling to us now? What will our buildings and gatherings physically create to reflect the revelation of this reformation? There will be exploration of new types of communication that will better facilitate family, in large and small settings. Greater anointing will result as an atmosphere is created that lines up with the message being communicated. We will move out of just preaching the need for family to modeling family; not just in a private setting, but in a public setting as well.

12. These two views of God listed below are key to embracing and sustaining this revelation. We must see God this way and also must have encountered Him personally in this manner if we are to step into the new role for the sons and daughters.

    a. Dad, the approachable, fun, kind, loving, strong, protector, provider, tenderhearted and nurturing one.

    b. Jesus, our husband who is looking into our eyes affectionately holding our hands and gently speaking in conversation with us, his bride.

13. Out of these two God identities, our heavenly persona will emerge:

    a. We are people of light who carry the Father's heart. Therefore, we are approachable, fun loving, and yet strong protectors of those in our care. We are nurturing providers with generosity.

    b. We are the bride receiving the love of a good King and with gentle eyes tenderly speaking to people with kind words.

Upon manifesting the nature of God in our identities, then a greater harvest will certainly come. When Jesus walked the earth, many people were attracted to the light and acceptance that He exuded. As we are walking in the light of God and Jesus is shining through us, a greater harvest will certainly come.

Let the Reformation Begin!!!

Keith

ABOUT THE AUTHOR

Keith Ferrante is a 3rd generation pastor who travels internationally speaking in churches, conferences, ministry schools, and other venues. Keith carries a message of reform with a core foundations of joy, freedom, and family. He is a prophetic voice who carries a breaker anointing to open up the heavens and bringing timely corporate words. Keith carries the heart of the Father and has a passion to equip the body of Christ for work of the ministry with kingdom influence, in and outside of the church.

Keith and his wife, Heather, are currently on the leadership team of The Mission, in Vacaville, CA. Prior to that, they spent ten years as Senior Leaders at Shiloh Gateway of Worship in Willits, California. They have shown a consistent lifestyle of walking out what they teach and impart. Over the past several years they have overseen, planted, and worked with a variety of ministry schools in the United States and internationally. They carry an anointing to break heavens open over churches, regions, and nations through presence based ministry, prophetic teaching, and impartation. They have traveled to many nations bringing people into radical encounters with God. People experience joy, freedom, deliverance, healing and the love of God in their meetings.

Made in the USA
San Bernardino, CA
11 January 2015